SCHOLARSHIP IN WOMEN'S HISTORY: REDISCOVERED AND NEW

Editor

GERDA LERNER

A CARLSON PUBLISHING SERIES

For a complete listing of the titles in this series,
please see the back of this book.

An Improved Woman

THE WISCONSIN FEDERATION OF WOMEN'S CLUBS, 1895-1920

Janice C. Steinschneider

CARLSON
Publishing Inc

BROOKLYN, NEW YORK, 1994

Please see the end of this volume for a listing of all the titles in the Carlson Publishing Series *Scholarship in Women's History: Rediscovered and New*, edited by Gerda Lerner, of which this is Volume 10.

Library of Congress Cataloging-in-Publication Data

Steinschneider, Janice C., 1960-
    An improved woman: the Wisconsin Federation of Women's Clubs, 1895-1920 / by Janice C. Steinschneider.
       p. cm. — (Scholarship in women's history ; 10)
    Includes bibliographical references and index.
    ISBN 0-926019-71-6
    1. Wisconsin Federation of Women's Clubs—History.   2. Women—Wisconsin--Societies and clubs—History. I. Title II. Series: Scholarship in women's history ; 10

HQ1905.W6S74   1994
305.4'06'0775—dc20   94-18183

Typographic design: Julian Waters

Typeface: Bitstream ITC Galliard

Jacket and Case design: Alison Lew

Index prepared by Scholars Editorial Services, Inc., Madison, Wisconsin.

Printed on acid-free, 250-year-life paper.

Manufactured in the United States of America.

Contents

Editor's Introduction
to the Series

An important aspect of the development of modern scholarship in Women's History has been the recovery of lost, forgotten or neglected sources. In the 1960s, when the practitioners of Women's History were so few as to be virtually invisible to the general profession, one of the commonly heard answers to the question, why is there nothing about women in your text? was that, unfortunately, women until the most recent past, had to be counted among the illiterate and had therefore not left many sources. It was common then to refer to women as among the "anonymous"—a group that included members of minority racial and ethnic groups of both sexes, most working-class people, colonials, Native Americans and women. In short, most of the populations of the past. These ignorant and erroneous answers satisfied only those who wished to stifle discussion, but they did make the issue of "sources" an urgent concern to practitioners of Women's History.

To historians who had done work in primary sources regarding women, it was obvious that the alleged dearth of sources did not exist, but it was true that the sources were not readily available. In archives and finding guides, women disappeared under the names of male family members. The voluminous records of their organizational work were disorganized, uncatalogued, and not infrequently rotting in file boxes in basement storage rooms. Since few if any researchers were interested in them, there seemed to be little purpose in making them accessible or even maintaining them. There were no archival projects to preserve the primary sources of American women comparable to the well-supported archival projects concerning Presidents and male political leaders. There were only a few and quite partial bibliographies of American women, while the encyclopedic reference works, such as the *DAB* (*Dictionary of American Biography*) or similar sources traditionally neglected to include all but a small number of women notables.

When the three-volume *Notable American Women: 1607–1950: A Biographical Dictionary* appeared in 1971, (to be followed by a fourth volume in 1980), it marked an important contribution to sources on women.[1] This comprehensive scholarly work consisted of 1,801 entries, with a biographical essay and a bibliography of works by and about each woman under discussion. It readily became obvious to even the casual user of these volumes how few modern biographies of these notable women existed, despite the availability of sources.

The real breakthrough regarding "sources" was made by a "grand manuscript search," begun in 1971, which aimed to survey historical archives in every state and identify their holdings pertaining to women. This project was started by a small committee—Clarke Chambers, Carl Degler, Janet James, Anne Firor Scott and myself. After a mail questionnaire survey of 11,000 repositories in every state, to which more than 7,000 repositories responded, it was clear that the sources on women were far wider and deeper than anyone had suspected. Ultimately, the survey resulted in a two-volume reference tool, Andrea Hinding, ed., *Women's History Sources: A Guide to Archives and Manuscript Collections in the United States.*[2]

The project proved that there were unused and neglected sources of Women's History to be found literally in every archive in the country. Participation in the survey convinced many archivists to reorganize and reclassify their holdings, so that materials about women could be more readily identified.

The arguments about "illiterate women" and absence of sources are no longer heard, but the problem of having accessible sources for Women's History continued. Even after archives and libraries reorganized and reclassified their source holding on the subject, most of the pertinent materials were not available in print. Many of the early developers of Women's History worked on source collections, reprint edition projects and, of course, bibliographies. The rapid and quite spectacular expansion of the field brought with it such great demand for sources that publishers at last responded. The past twenty years have seen a virtual flood of publications in Women's History, so that the previous dearth of material seems almost inconceivable to today's students.

For myself, having put a good many years of my professional life into the development of "source books" and bibliographies, it did not seem particularly urgent to continue the effort under the present conditions. But I was awakened to the fact that there might still be a problem of neglected and forgotten sources in Women's History as a result of a conference, which Kathryn Sklar and I organized in 1988. The Wingspread Conference "Graduate Training in U.S. Women's History" brought together 63 representatives of 57 institutions of higher education who each represented a graduate program in Women's History. As part of our preparation for the conference, we asked each person invited to list all the dissertations in Women's History she had directed or was then directing. The result was staggering: it appeared that there were 99 completed dissertations and 236 then underway. This was by no means the entire national output, since we surveyed only the 63 participants at the conference and did not survey the many faculty persons not represented, who had directed such dissertations. The questions arose—What happened to all these dissertations? Why did so many of them not get published?

When Ralph Carlson approached me at about that time with the idea of publishing "lost sources" in Women's History, I was more ready than I would have been without benefit of the Wingspread survey to believe that, indeed, there still were some such neglected sources out there, and to undertake such a project.

We used the dissertation list from the Wingspread Conference as a starting point. A researcher then went through all the reference works listing dissertations in history and other fields in the English language from 1870 to the present. Among these she identified 1,235 titles in what we now call Women's History. We then cross-checked these titles against the electronic catalog of the Library of Congress, which represents every book owned by the LC (or to define it differently, every book copyrighted and published in the U.S.). This cross-check revealed that of the 1,235 dissertations, 314 had been published, which is more than 25 percent. That represents an unusually high publication ratio, which may be a reflection of the growth and quality of the field.

A further selection based on abstracts of the 921 unpublished dissertations narrowed the field to 101. Of these we could not locate 33 authors or the authors were not interested in publication. Out of the 68 remaining dissertations we selected the eleven we considered best in both scholarship and writing. These are first-rate books that should have been published earlier and that for one reason or another fell between the cracks.

Why did they not get published earlier? In the case of the Boatwright manuscript, an unusually brilliant Master's thesis done in 1939, undoubtedly the neglect of Women's History at that time made the topic seem unsuitable for publication. Similar considerations may have worked against publication of several other earlier dissertations. In other cases, lack of mentorship and inexperience discouraged the writers from pursuing publication in the face of one or two rejections of their manuscripts. Several of the most valuable books in the series required considerable rewriting under editorial supervision, which, apparently, had not earlier been available to the authors. There are also several authors who became members of what we call "the lost generation," historians getting their degrees in the 1980s when there were few jobs available. This group of historians, which disproportionately consisted of women, retooled and went into different fields. Three of the books in this series are the work of these historians, who needed considerable persuasion to do the necessary revisions and editing. We are pleased to have found their works and to have persisted in the effort of making them available to a wider readership, since they have a distinct contribution to make.

The books in this series cover a wide range of topics. Two of them are detailed studies in the status of women, one in Georgia, 1783-1860, the other in Russia in the early 1900s. Two are valuable additions to the literature on the anti-woman's suffrage campaigns in the U.S. Of the four books dealing with the history of women's organizations, three are detailed regional studies and one is a comparative history of the British and American Women's Trade Union League. Finally, the three biographical studies of eighteenth- and nineteenth-century women offer either new information or new interpretations of their subjects.

Eleanor Miot Boatwright, *Status of Women in Georgia, 1783–1860*, was discovered by Professor Anne Firor Scott in the Duke University archives and represents, in her words "a buried treasure." An M.A. thesis written by a high school teacher in Augusta, Georgia, its level of scholarship and the depth of its research are of the quality expected of a dissertation. The author has drawn on a vast range of primary sources, including legal sources that were then commonly used for social history, to document and analyze the social customs, class differences, work and religion of white women in Georgia. While her treatment of race relations reflects the limitations of scholarship on that subject in the 1930s, she gives careful attention to the impact of race relations on white women. Her analysis of the linkage made by Southern male apologists for slavery between the subordination ("protection") of women and the subordination of slaves (also rationalized as their "protection") is particularly insightful. The work has much information to offer the contemporary scholar and can be compared in its scholarship and its general approach to the work of Julia Spruill and Elizabeth Massey. When it is evaluated in comparison with other social histories of its period, its research methodology and interpretative focus on women are truly remarkable.

Anne Bobroff-Hajal's, *Working Women in Russia Under the Hunger Tsars: Political Activism and Daily Life*, is a fascinating, excellently researched study of a topic on which there is virtually no material available in the English language. Focusing on women industrial workers in Russia's Central Industrial Region, most of them employed in textile production, Bobroff studied their daily lives and family patterns, their gender socialization, their working and living conditions and their political activism during the Revolution: in political organizations, in food riots and in street fighting. The fact that these women and their families lived mostly in factory barracks will be of added interest to labor historians, who may wish to compare their lives and activities with other similarly situated groups in the U.S. and England. Drawing on a rich mixture of folkloric sources, local newspapers, oral histories, workers' memoirs and ethnographic material, Bobroff presents a convincing and intimate picture of working-class life before the Russian Revolution. Bobroff finds that the particularly strong mother-child bonding of Russian women workers, to which they were indoctrinated from childhood on, undermined their ability to form coherent political groups capable of maintaining their identity over a long period of time. Her thesis, excellently supported and well argued, may undermine some commonly held beliefs on this subject. It should prove of interest to all scholars working on gender socialization and to others working on labor culture, working-class activism, and class consciousness.

Rosemary Keller, *Patriotism and the Female Sex: Abigail Adams and the American Revolution*, is a sophisticated, well-documented interpretation of Abigail Adams's intellectual and political development, set firmly within the historical context. Compared with other Abigail Adams biographies, this work is outstanding in treating her seriously as an agent in history and as an independent intellectual. Abigail Adams emerges from this study as a woman going as far as it was possible to go within the limits of the gender conventions of her time and struggling valiantly, through influencing her husband, to extend these gender conventions. This is an accomplishment quite sufficient for one woman's life time. Professor Keller's sensitive biography makes a real contribution to colonial and women's history.

Elizabeth Ann Bartlett, *Liberty, Equality, Sorority: The Origins and Integrity of Feminist Thought: Frances Wright, Sarah Grimké and Margaret Fuller*, is another work of intellectual history. It attempts to define a common "feminism" emerging from the thought of these important nineteenth-century thinkers and concludes that feminism, in order to sustain itself, must balance the tensions between the concepts of liberty, equality, and sorority. The lucid, well-researched discussions of each woman's life and work should appeal to the general reader and make this book a valuable addition to courses in intellectual history and women's history and literature.

Mary Grant, *Private Woman, Public Person: An Account of the Life of Julia Ward Howe from 1819 to 1868*, is a sensitive, feminist study of Howe's life and thought up to the turning point in 1868, when she decided to dedicate her life to public activism in behalf of women. By carefully analyzing Howe's private letters and journals, the author uncovers a freer, more powerful and creative writer beneath the formal *persona* of the author of "The Battle Hymn of the Republic" than we have hitherto known. She also discusses in detail Howe's fascinating, never published, unfinished novel, "Eva and Raphael," which features a number of then taboo subjects, such as rape, madness and an androgynous character. This well-written biography reveals new aspects and dimensions of Julia Ward Howe's life and work.

Jane Jerome Camhi, *Women Against Women: American Anti-Suffragism, 1880-1920*, and Thomas J. Jablonsky, *The Home, Heaven, and Mother Party: Female Anti-Suffragists in America, 1868-1920*, are complementary studies that should be indispensable for any serious student or scholar of woman suffrage. They are, in fact, the only extant book-length studies of anti-suffragism. This important movement has until now been accessible to modern readers only through the somewhat biased lens of contemporary suffragists' observations. They consistently underestimated its scope and significance and did not engage with its basic paradox, that it was a movement by women against women.

Jane Camhi's comprehensive study of nationwide anti-woman's suffrage movements makes this paradox a central theme. Camhi analyses the "antis' " ideas and ideology and offers some thought-provoking theories about the competing and contradictory positions women took in regard to formal political power. Her insightful profile of a noted anti-suffragist, Ida Tarbell, is an additional contribution this fine book makes to the historical literature.

Thomas Jablonsky's study is focused more narrowly on the organizational history of the rise and fall of the movement. The book is based on extensive research in the organizational records of the anti-suffragists on a state and national level, the records of Congressional hearings, biographical works and the manuscripts of leaders. Jablonsky takes the "antis" seriously and disproves the suffragists' argument that they were merely pawns of male interest groups. He offers a sympathetic, but critical evaluation of their ideas. His detailed attention to organizational efforts in states other than the major battle-grounds—Massachusetts, New York and Illinois—make this book a valuable resource for scholars in history, political science and Women's History.

The four remaining books in the series all focus on aspects of women's organizational activities. Taken together, they reveal the amazing energy, creativity, and persistence of women's institution building on the community and local level. They sustain and highlight the thesis that women built the infrastructures of community life, while men held the positions of visible power. Based on research in four distinctly different regions, these studies should prove useful not only for the intrinsic worth of each, but for comparative purposes.

Darlene Roth, *Matronage: Patterns in Women's Organizations, Atlanta, Georgia, 1890-1940*, is a thoroughly researched, gracefully written study of the networks of women's organizations in that city. The author's focus on conservative women's organizations, such as the Daughters of the American Revolution, the Colonial Dames, and the African-American Chatauqua Circle, adds to the significance of the book. The author defines "matronage" as the functions and institutionalization of the networks of social association among women. By focusing on a Southern city in the Progressive era, Roth provides rich comparative material for the study of women's voluntarism. She challenges notions of the lack of organizational involvement by Southern women. She traces the development of women's activities from communal service orientation—the building of war memorials—to advocacy of the claims of women and children and, finally, to advocacy of women's rights. Her comparative approach, based on the study of the records of white and African-American women's organizations and leadership—she studied 508 white and 150 black women—is illuminating and offers new insights. The book should be of interest to readers in Urban and Community History, Southern History, and Women's History.

Robin Miller Jacoby, *The British and American Women's Trade Union Leagues, 1890-1925: A Case Study of Feminism and Class*, is a comparative study of working-class women in Britain and America in the Progressive period. Although parts of this work have appeared as articles in scholarly journals, the work has never before been accessible in its entirety. Jacoby traces the development of Women's Trade Union Leagues in Britain and America, exploring their different trajectories and settings. By focusing on the interaction of women's and labor movements, the author provides rich empirical material. Her analysis of the tensions and overlapping interests of feminism and class consciousness is important to feminist theory. Her discussion of protective labor legislation, as it was debated and acted upon in two different contexts, makes an important contribution to the existing literature. It also addressees issues still topical and hotly debated in the present day. The book will be of interest to labor historians, Women's History specialists, and the general public.

Janice Steinschneider, *An Improved Woman: The Wisconsin Federation of Women's Clubs, 1895-1920*, is a richly documented study based on a multitude of primary sources, which reveals the amazing range of women's activities as community builders and agents of change. Wisconsin clubwomen founded libraries, fostered changes in school curricula and worked to start kindergartens and playgrounds. They helped preserve historic and natural landmarks and organized to improve public health services. They built a sound political base—long before they had the right of suffrage—from which they trained women leaders for whom they then helped to secure public appointments. They worked to gain access for women to university education and employment and, in addition to many other good causes, they worked for world peace. Steinschneider's description and analysis of "women's public sphere" is highly sophisticated. Hers is one of the best studies on the subject and should prove indispensable to all concerned with understanding women's political activities, their construction of a public sphere for women, and their efforts and successes as builders of large coalitions.

Margit Misangyi Watts, *High Tea at Halekulani: Feminist Theory and American Clubwomen*, is a more narrowly focused study of clubwomen's work than are the other three, yet its significance ranges far above that of its subject matter. Watts tells the story of the Outdoor Circle, an upper-class white women's club in Hawaii, from its founding in 1911 on. Its main activities were to make Hawaii beautiful: to plant trees, clean up eyesores, preserve nature and rid the islands of billboards. To achieve these modest goals, the women had to become consummate politicians and lobbyists and learn how to run grassroots boycotts and publicity and educational campaigns, and how to form long-lasting coalitions. Above all, as Watts's fine theoretical analysis shows, they insisted that their female vision, their woman-centered view, become an accepted part of the public discourse. This case study is rich in theoretical implications. Together with the other three studies of women's club activities it offers not only a wealth of practical examples of women's work for social change, but it also shows that such work both resists patriarchal views and practices and redefines them in the interests of women.

Gerda Lerner
Madison, Wisconsin

List of Illustrations

(All photographs are from the State Historical Society of Wisconsin)

An Improved Woman

ONE

The Woman's Club Movement, 1868-1920: History and Historiography

Nineteenth-century gender role ideology firmly placed women in the private, domestic realm. Yet, after the Civil War, increasingly large numbers of women took part in public activities. Contemporaries noted this surge in women's public participation, calling it the Woman Movement. Organizations were one important locus of women's public activity. Women joined, for instance, the Woman's Christian Temperance Union, the Association of Collegiate Alumnae (later the American Association of University Women), suffrage associations, settlements, and, by the turn of the century, the National Consumers' League and the National Women's Trade Union League.

Another set of women's organizations constituted the woman's club movement. With memberships of a dozen to several hundred, women's clubs had a variety of activities and purposes. Many were affiliated in a large national organization called the General Federation of Women's Clubs. The woman's club movement has the distinction of being one of the earliest mass movements of American women, the General Federation approaching the one-million-member mark shortly after 1910.[1] Many more women were members of clubs that were unfederated.

Given its mass appeal, surprisingly little historical interpretation of the woman's club movement exists. Club members were often quite interested in

1

the history of their organizations, and so they have written numerous descriptive histories of individual clubs and state federations, many of them unpublished and housed in club archives. National leaders of the club movement have written several histories of the national movement.[2]

Historian Karen Blair wrote the first full scholarly treatment of the woman's club movement informed by the modern feminist movement. Blair argues that in clubs, women could "increase autonomy, assert sorority, win education, and seize influence . . . in the forbidden public sphere."[3] The woman's club movement had an important impact on the lives of many women and is a promising subject for historians interested in women between the Civil War and the woman suffrage victory in 1920.

Although women's religious, benevolent, and reform organizations existed throughout the antebellum period, both contemporaries and modern historians mark the beginning of the woman's club movement in 1868, when two of the most well-known and influential women's clubs were born.

Sorosis, one of these two stellar clubs, originated in New York City, meeting first in April 1868. It was founded at the instigation of Jane Cunningham Croly, a journalist and later a key figure in the club movement. The immediate impetus to Croly's action was an incident of sex discrimination. When Croly applied for a ticket to a dinner held by the Press Club of New York, in honor of Charles Dickens, she was refused—because she was a woman. Croly, and the women who joined her in Sorosis, created something rather unusual: a secular organization of women, who came together for general, mutual support and self-development. The charter of Sorosis specified its purposes:

> the promotion of agreeable and useful relations among women of literary, artistic and scientific tastes; the discussion and dissemination of principles and facts which promise to exert a salutary influence on women and on society; and the establishment of an order which shall render the female sex helpful to each other, and actively benevolent in the world.[4]

The frustration that led Croly to found Sorosis must have been felt by many women, and the club must have fulfilled many of their needs, for Sorosis became popular. Beginning with twelve women, Sorosis's membership topped eighty a year later, and it continued to grow. Sorosis drew its membership from the corps of New York's professional women: Authors, journalists, artists, teachers, editors, physicians, lawyers, and ministers all participated.[5]

The "benevolent to the world" clause of Sorosis's charter notwithstanding, most of its activities involved education of its members through lectures, the presentation of papers, and discussion. At first, cultural concerns such as literature and art occupied much of the members' time.[6] But interest quickly expanded, so that by 1898, Sorosis had eight standing committees: literature, science, education, art, philanthropy, house and home, drama, and current events.[7] And from the beginning, the members of Sorosis were interested in other women, reflecting a high degree of gender consciousness. For example, club members' study of art included consideration of women artists and artists' portrayals of women.[8]

Sorosis's concentration on the self-interest and personal growth of its members drew criticism from the public and the media. Indeed, since the true woman was supposed to be self-denying and self-sacrificing, the program of Sorosis had certain radical implications. Despite this criticism, Sorosis was safe for nonradical, somewhat conservative women to join. Its members emphasized their ladylike, respectable qualities, and following the lead of Croly, were quick to disassociate Sorosis from those wild-eyed radicals—the suffragists. Many members in fact were suffrage supporters, but this controversial issue was carefully avoided during the early years of the club, thus uniting in one group women of varying political opinions.[9]

The New England Woman's Club also first met in 1868. Founded by Caroline Severance, the club drew its membership from Boston's reformist and philanthropic community. Unlike Sorosis, men were allowed to join, but control of the organization was in the hands of its women members, who also dominated numerically.[10] Suffragist Julia Ward Howe, like Croly a key figure in the club movement, belonged to the New England Woman's Club.

Like Sorosis, the New England Woman's Club offered its members opportunities for self-development, sisterhood, and support. The education of its members was one of the chief works of this club, too, and in true reformist spirit, an eclectic range of modern ideas got a hearing.[11] But unlike their sisters in Sorosis, from the beginning these reforming New England women used their club to translate creative ideas into practice. Together club members undertook a variety of projects. For example, in the early 1870s, they campaigned for women's election to the Boston Public School Board and successfully helped support the establishment of Girls Latin School in Boston. In 1874, stimulated by an address on dress reform, the club opened a store selling dress reform clothing. From 1870 to 1878, the club maintained a horticulture school for women.

During the last three decades of the nineteenth century, women founded and joined women's clubs throughout the country, in small villages and large cities. Sorosis and the New England Woman's Club are not entirely representative of such clubs. The members of most clubs tended to be middle-aged married women leading ordinary, domestic lives, not the professionals of Sorosis or the prominent reformers of the NEWC. A satisfying, comprehensive explanation of this simultaneous springing up of clubs is lacking. Some scholars trace women's clubs to the newfound leisure of middle-class women.[12] Blair argues that middle-aged educated women, who were reaching significant numbers in these years, joined women's clubs to invigorate their tedious, disappointing, domestically circumscribed lives.[13] Whatever the cause, the widespread appearance of women's clubs demonstrates that they fulfilled a real need. The majority of these clubs can be placed in three categories: the self-improvement club (also study, literary, or culture club), the department club, and the civic club.

Most women's clubs were self-improvement clubs. These often had small memberships, a dozen or so women who met to educate themselves. At club meetings members presented papers, and discussion followed. Frequently, the club chose an annual topic, and study done for the year concentrated on that topic.

In general, clubwomen favored subjects like literature, art, history, religion, and broad studies of particular nations. The Tuesday Club of Fort Atkinson, Wisconsin, for instance, reported studying, from its inception in 1880 to 1898, both history and literature, especially pre-Shakespearean drama, Shakespeare, and modern American and English literature.[14] But the interests of self-improvement clubs frequently spread beyond these somewhat traditional subjects into science, social science, philosophy, and current events. For example, the eighth district vice president of the Wisconsin Federation of Women's Clubs reported at the 1899 convention that, "The Kewaunee Shakespeare Club has added to its study of Shakespeare the subjects of child-study and factory employment of children."[15] And, as in Sorosis, club topics often exemplified a high degree of gender consciousness; clubwomen were interested in women's rights, responsibilities, and opportunities.[16]

Frequently, clubwomen's interests expanded beyond self-education, and they took up practical projects. For example, the Woman's Club of Kaukauna, Wisconsin, organized in 1897, had three stated goals in its constitution: "the intellectual development of its members"; "a spirit of social harmony and mutual helpfulness"; and "the establishment of a public library in the city."

This latter goal was achieved in 1905.[17] At about the same time, the Ideal Club of Waukesha combined the study of Scandinavia, home economics, and music, with the operation of an emergency hospital.[18]

Department clubs were much larger than self-improvement clubs and usually were associated with cities rather than towns. Contemporaries considered the department club a more modern innovation.[19] The department club comprised several semi-autonomous departments or committees, each with its own line of work. Each department arranged for the study of its particular subject, and, as in self-improvement clubs, such study frequently led to civic projects. The Madison Woman's Club was one of Wisconsin's best-known clubs. Organized as a study club in 1892, its membership grew rapidly, and a few years later the club reorganized its standing committees into seven departments: art, history, social, music, literature, education, and philanthropy. By the end of its first decade, with two hundred members, the Madison Woman's Club had established a solid record in social service. It had successfully agitated for larger appropriations for the primary and kindergarten departments of the city schools; given art collections to the schools and the Wisconsin Free Library Commission; supplied clothing to poor families; established a sewing class for poor children; organized a citywide associated charities; helped get home economics and industrial arts classes in the schools; begun a fund-raising drive for a city hospital; and inaugurated a campaign to improve the sanitary conditions of city streets.[20]

Like the department club, the development of the civic club was a later phase in the woman's club movement. Women who joined civic clubs took up the task of municipal improvement and worked to better the services, facilities, and amenities of their communities. The Philadelphia Civic Club, organized in 1893, was one of the first. In its first five years, it improved the physical plant of city schools, secured more adequate disposal of household waste, and encouraged Philadelphians to improve their care of their cellars. In 1896, it launched the Octavia Hill Association, a joint stock company whose purpose was to buy, renovate, and then rent housing in poor neighborhoods.[21] The River Falls (Wisconsin) Improvement League, organized in 1900, cleared the city of weeds and litter, and converted dumping grounds into parks. In 1913, it opened a public rest room for women.[22]

Although many of the projects undertaken by women's clubs may seem petty and insignificant today, their work, taken as a whole, significantly altered the nature of American communities. By World War I, women's clubs were working in a wide variety of fields—for example, education, public health, social service, civic improvement, libraries, and the conditions of women and children. Clubwomen were instrumental in the introduction of kindergartens, home economics, industrial arts, summer schools, and night schools into American education. Many clubs undertook projects to improve the physical plant of schools, by decorating classrooms and setting up playgrounds. Others ventured into cleaning streets, beautifying railroad stations and town landscapes, and pressing for better municipal sanitation. Many clubwomen founded or supported free public libraries; others preserved local historical landmarks or agitated for the protection of natural resources. Some undertook studies of working conditions, food purity, or infant mortality in their communities. The flexibility of women's clubs was an important feature of the club movement. It attracted women with diverse interests and offered them access to work in any number of fields that were important to them.

And women's clubs used a range of methods to achieve their goals. Members raised funds, ran community events and projects, lobbied for (or against) particular laws, sponsored and carried out investigations, served as public officials and inspectors; educated the public at large, and established and maintained institutions. Frequently, institutions begun by women's clubs were taken over by municipal authorities. This, in conjunction with the legislation women's clubs supported, helped change American ideas about the extent of government responsibilities.[23]

As clubwomen changed their communities, they changed themselves. Club work encouraged the growth of a conscious sense of sisterhood, and in this supportive atmosphere, women's clubs helped their members acquire new skills and refurbish those grown rusty. For instance, self-improvement clubs taught women to write more skillfully, to speak in public, and to think more clearly, although study in such clubs often did not meet the most rigorous of intellectual standards. Similarly, women who worked on their club's civic ventures gained new abilities and a positive self-awareness. When Blair emphasizes the significance of the skills and ensuing self-confidence women developed in their clubs, she echoes the sentiments of many of these women.[24]

Another organizational expression of the woman's club movement took form in the last decade of the nineteenth century. Individual clubs began to affiliate with one another in regional, state, and national federations. Clubwomen organized the General Federation of Women's Clubs (GFWC), a national organization, in 1890, with Jane Croly and her fellow Sorosis members leading the way. The ambitious Croly sought a centralized, national association, an alliance of clubs that would increase clubwomen's power and influence. In 1889, Sorosis invited ninety-seven clubs to meet in New York, both to celebrate Sorosis's twenty-first anniversary and to discuss the past, present, and future of the woman's club movement. More than sixty clubs sent delegates, and at this meeting the idea for a national federation began to take shape. The first meeting of the General Federation took place in 1890, and in 1892 the Federation held the first of its biennial conventions.[25] Although not all women's clubs joined the GFWC, the organization grew steadily. From an initial fifty-one charter members, it had a membership of 495 clubs, representing 100,000 women, in 1896. By 1900, the Federation had more than 150,000 members; in 1914, it passed one million.[26]

In the beginning, by the terms of its constitution, the GFWC was an alliance of self-education clubs, although Federation members understood that this did not in any way prohibit these clubs for involvement in more public concerns. But prominent clubwomen, such as Croly, pursued their goal of using the GFWC to increase women's public power. Beginning in the early years of the Federation, these women applied gentle but firm pressure to move the GFWC and individual clubs in this direction, stimulating a natural impulse. In 1896, the Federation constitution was changed, permitting nonstudy clubs to join.[27] Department clubs had been welcome from the beginning, so long as one of their main activities was self-improvement.

The growth of the roster of the General Federation's standing committees illustrates the expanding concerns of the GFWC. At the earliest conventions, club methods for self-education were the primary interest of the participants. But at the 1896 convention, committees made their first appearance, under the headings of literature, education, home philanthropy, and social economics. At the 1898 convention, a civic committee, an industrial committee, and a committee on libraries appeared. By 1902, the Federation had organized a forestry committee.[28] In 1906, the following committees reported to the convention: art, child labor, civic, civil service reform, education, forestry, household economics, industrial, legislative, library extension, literature, and pure food. The list of committees remained substantially the same until World War I, except that by 1912, the Federation had organized conservation and public health committees. And in 1916, there was a peace committee. In its first twenty-five years, the General Federation's evolving concerns reflected and encouraged a similar progression among clubwomen generally.[29]

The GFWC frequently expressed interest in the conditions of women. One of its first resolutions, passed at the 1894 convention, condemned the double standard of sexual morality and demanded that men live up to the same

7

standards that were required of women. At the 1898 convention, at which delegates heard Beatrice Webb and Jane Addams speak on the "Industrial Problems of Women and Children," Federation members passed a resolution favoring maximum work hours for women (and children). In 1910, the GFWC began compiling a compendium of state laws relevant to the legal rights of women. Two years later, the GFWC passed resolutions supporting legislation to equalize women's position in marriage, protect widows from poverty, and aid women whose husbands had deserted them.[30]

Taken as a whole, the resolutions passed by the Federation exemplify the eclectic exuberance of GFWC interests. Federation delegates expressed their opinions on, for instance, child labor, education, conservation, industrial problems, pure food, and civic conditions. The GFWC became an effective lobby for progressive legislation, and resolutions often embodied support for particular proposed laws.

Leading clubwomen used Federation machinery to prod state federations and individual clubs. The committees suggested new topics of interest to clubs; these committees and Federation officers sent letters to clubs urging them to act along particular lines. In 1906, the civic committee of GFWC compiled and sent to all Federation clubs a manual called *A Civic Planner*, suggesting practical programs for civic improvement. GFWC officers and representatives attended state federation meetings to explain and generate enthusiasm for GFWC goals and projects.[31]

Clubwomen replicated the organization of the GFWC at the state level. The clubwomen of Maine led the way, organizing the Maine Federation of Women's Clubs in 1892. By 1900, more than thirty states had federations, and by 1911, every state had one.[32] Initially, GFWC leaders feared competition from state federation, but in 1894 the Board of Directors of the GFWC began to support the formation of state federations and encouraged them, successfully, to join the General Federation.[33]

Like the GFWC, state federations developed wide-ranging interests, although each tended to emphasize its particular set of chief concerns. During the first thirty years of state federation development, they were especially drawn to ventures involving education, libraries, civic improvement, conservation, preservation and development of natural and historical landmarks, juvenile courts, and public health. State federations often owned traveling libraries and established scholarships.[34]

Thus, throughout the United States women united in clubs based on a sense of shared womanhood. But such sentiments were not sufficient to overcome certain major social barriers, especially that of race. Nationally, most women's clubs did not accept black women; consequently, black women formed their own clubs. The race issue was controversial and divisive within the General Federation. In 1900, the inadvertent admission of a black club to the GFWC touched off an internal conflict. Federation leaders realized that the admission of black clubs risked the continued membership of white, southern clubs. In 1902, a "compromise" was reached, effectively excluding black clubs from the GFWC. Black clubwomen supported their own federation, the National Association of Colored Women, established in 1896.[35]

The black woman's club movement was at once similar to and different from its white counterpart. Gerda Lerner has noted that black clubwomen were inspired in part by the successes of white clubwomen. Black women also used their clubs for both the improvement of self and the improvement of the community. But black clubwomen responded particularly to the special needs of their race. They worked for the protection and advancement of black people and the nurturing of race pride. Frequently, they established community institutions; in a racist society, the existing institutions failed to serve the black community. And many of the services provided by black clubwomen were designed to ameliorate the widespread poverty of the black community, that resulted from economic discrimination.[36]

Despite the racism within the woman's club movement, its accomplishments are impressive. Clubwomen provided a range of significant services to their communities. These women were an integral part of Americans' response to the problems posed by urban industrial development. And the club movement introduced a large number of women to public activities traditionally proscribed to them. The expansion of women's public opportunities and life choices is a goal we readily identify with feminism. And when explicitly celebrating sisterhood and working to improve the lives of women, women's clubs demonstrated the gender consciousness that is part of any feminist movement.

Nevertheless, the woman's club movement occupies an ambiguous place in the feminist wave of the late nineteenth and early twentieth centuries. Clubwomen were by and large middle-class, and their movement had a distinctly conventional tone to it. Clubwomen usually supported traditional notions about women's domestic role and special womanly character. The rhetoric of clubwomen and the GFWC was replete with images of motherhood, the home, and women's special mission. Furthermore, the

GFWC did not endorse woman suffrage until 1914, for fear of losing its more conservative members, especially the southern women.[37]

Despite the complexity, popularity, and significant achievements of the woman's club movement, scholars have left it relatively unexplored. In the works that do treat women's clubs, two major themes emerge: the effects women's clubs had on the community, and the effects women's clubs had on women. In general, works treating the club movement emphasize one of these themes. Most of the recent scholarship on the club movement, which emphasizes the issue of women's clubs' significance for women, explicitly explores the relationship of the club movement to feminism. These works will be discussed together.

Mary Beard's *Woman's Work in Municipalities*, published in 1915, was one of the first serious treatments of women's clubs. Beard's chief concern was the effect the clubs had on their communities. She documented the presence of women in the public sphere of city and town life, the women's contribution to the shaping and progressive reform of modern urban structures, institutions, and customs. Beard's work portrays women in a variety of roles: as professionals, private individuals, residents of settlements, and members of bureaus, boards, and women's clubs. She demonstrated that women in women's clubs successfully changed their communities in ways they thought desirable, working in a broad range of different areas and through a variety of different methods. Beard referred to the effect of women's clubs' work on women themselves much more cursorily. It is clear that she believed that such clubs were helping women find the power to act in and change the public sphere.[38]

Beard's book is difficult for the historian to work with. Highly descriptive, it offers little comprehensive interpretation of women's participation in community work. Here and there, Beard suggested that women took up particular community projects by way of following their traditional concerns into the community. Thus, she argued, women, traditionally responsible for children, naturally sought to improve schools. Their housekeeping responsibilities led them to a concern with the cleanliness of community streets; their responsibility for the family's food led them to support the pure food movement.[39] Occasionally, Beard noted that the greater leisure of middle-class women relative to both the lower class and to middle-class men left them with the time to become involved in community affairs.[40] Analytically thin, Beard's book also only infrequently gave exact dates for particular accomplishments of women and their clubs. *Woman's Work in Municipalities* has a somewhat ahistorical quality and cannot be used to trace the development of women's clubs.

Social worker and scholar Sophonisba Breckinridge, who wrote about women's clubs some fifteen years later than Beard, was concerned with issues relatively ignored by Beard. Breckinridge described and interpreted the development of the GFWC, which was for her the club movement writ large. Hence, the perspective of change that was undeveloped by Beard was explored by Breckinridge. She analyzed the GFWC within a larger discussion of women's organizations. Thus, the General Federation is one example of the overall tendency in the last decade of the nineteenth century for women's local organizations to federate and centralize into regional and national organizations. Then, in the first decade of the twentieth century, national women's organizations began consistent attempts at cooperation with one another and with other national organizations; the GFWC participated in this trend.[41]

Breckinridge's analysis differed from Beard's in another way. Although she recognized the success of women's community work, Breckinridge emphasized the significance of the club movement for the women involved in it. She believed that through clubs, women expressed their aspirations as they defined them. Indeed, she argued that changing concerns of clubwomen within the GFWC are an index to the changing goals and interests of "ordinary" women.[42]

Breckinridge identified a tension within the GFWC in relation to women's developing interest. Leaders in the club movement tended to have a greater desire than many of the rank-and-file members to move beyond study and pursue more practical projects. According to Breckinridge, self-improvement clubs remained in the majority within the Federation. And although there was a real tendency, regardless of the GFWC, for the work of self-improvement clubs to expand into public pursuits, leaders within the Federation worked hard to accelerate that process. Breckinridge showed that Federation leaders achieved real, but uneven, progress along these lines.[43]

In light of the re-emergence of a feminist movement in the past several decades, it is not surprising that modern historians have attempted to assess the woman's club movement in terms of its relationship to feminism in the late nineteenth and early twentieth centuries. William O'Neill initiated this discussion in 1969.[44] He sought to explain what he saw as "the failure of feminism," namely, why the feminists of fifty to one hundred years ago did not achieve a lasting equality. O'Neill attributed this failure of the development of social feminism, which linked feminist goals with a belief in women's special mission to reform the world. O'Neill's analysis is relevant to the woman's club movement because he placed women's clubs and the GFWC in the tradition of social feminism.

O'Neill's interpretation posited two key flaws in social feminism. First, social feminists failed to challenge any assumptions regarding the organization of society that were central to maintaining the status quo. Hence, social feminists developed no scheme for drastic reorganization of society along lines compatible with equality. Most damaging was the social feminists' acquiescence to traditional assumptions regarding the organization of the home and the family. As a result, they could not recognize that the roots of women's oppression lay in the organization of the domestic realm. Second, O'Neill criticized social feminists' relationship to social reform. He argued that in their eclectic support for a plethora of reforms, social feminists subordinated women's needs as women to the needs of society in general. Thus social feminists often lost sight of purely *feminist* goals because they believed in women's special responsibility to reform the country as a whole.

O'Neill's criticism of social feminists, and thus clubwomen, is a criticism of their ideology. Jill Conway's interpretation of women reformers from 1870 to 1930 involves a similar analysis.[45] Conway contrasts two different styles adopted by the feminist reformers of this period. The "professional expert" was a role theoretically appropriate for either sex. The "female sage or prophetess" was limited to women and justified women's right to criticize and reform society on the basis of feminine intuition and moral sensitivity. Conway argues that the female sage, the more popular style, fatally undercut the achievement of equality because it affirmed traditional notions about a special, female temperament. The analysis raises questions about the relationship between changes in behavior and changes in ideology. Conway notes that although the behavior of women reformers was very different from traditionally sanctioned behavior, their ideology did not change to make ideas and behavior "match up."

Conway's argument is germane to the women's club movement because for the most part clubwomen adopted the female sage style of reform. It is analogous to O'Neill's argument because it emphasizes the limitations of ideas elaborated by women reformers. Karen Blair's interpretation of the woman's club movement also focuses on questions of ideology. But Blair's conclusions are quite different from O'Neill's and Conway's. Where they see liabilities, Blair finds strengths.

To characterize the ideology of clubwomen, Blair borrows a term originally used by Daniel Scott Smith: "domestic feminism." Smith used the term to refer to what he saw as "women's increasing autonomy within the family" in the nineteenth century.[46] Blair's use of "domestic feminism" changes its meaning. Blair argues that domestic feminists selected particular aspects of the traditional image of the ideal woman and used them to justify women's participation in new activities. For example, the true woman was supposed to be more sensitive to culture (in the artistic, literary sense) than men; thus, women had a right to study culture and assert authority in matters of culture. Similarly, as women were better housekeepers than men, and the care of the city was essentially like the care of the home, women had a right and a duty to enter civic affairs. Clubwomen's special pride in feminine values may even have masked a certain degree of hostility to masculine values.[47]

According to Blair, the elaboration of domestic feminism, as she used the term, accounts for the broad appeal of the woman's club movement. Even conservative women could participate. Support for domestic feminism required a far less radical stance than did support for complete equality, as the former did not involve a blatant repudiation of the basic tenets of traditional sex-role ideology.[48] Hence, that which Blair finds especially valuable, Conway and O'Neill see as a flaw.

Blair's interpretation has its merits, particularly as it evaluates the woman's club movement in terms of what it did rather than what we wish it had done. But Blair's is perhaps a rosy, optimistic interpretation. When she notes that the GFWC endorsed woman suffrage in 1914, she does not emphasize that it took it so long to do so. Rather she enthusiastically construes this endorsement as a culmination of the feminist tendencies in the ideology elaborated by the club movement.[49] Blair tends also to overestimate the importance of the advancement of women in the General Federation's ideas and program, slighting ambiguities and ambivalence in the clubwomen's treatment of this issue. Finally, Blair recognizes, as did Breckinridge, the struggle within the GFWC regarding the shift from cultural to civic and political concerns. Once again, Blair has a more optimistic view, implying that the victory of the reformers in the club movement was virtually complete.[50]

Blair's positive evaluation of women's clubs, in relation to feminism, is shared by Estelle Freedman.[51] At the same time, Freedman, like O'Neill, is searching for an explanation for the decline of feminism following the victory of the suffragists. But Freedman's analysis differs from those of O'Neill, Conway, and Blair in that she moves well beyond questions of ideology.

Freedman is concerned with the structure of the woman movement, rather than with only its ideas. She observed the feminist strategy, from 1870 to 1920, of female institution building in women's clubs and the club federations, the Woman's Christian Temperance Union, women's colleges, settlements, the Women's Trade Union League, and the Consumers' League. A thriving women's culture, and the close, single-sex relationships it encouraged, gave strength to these feminine institutions, whose purpose, Freedman argues, was the construction of a separate but vital public sphere for women. Freedman sees the goal of creating a separate women's public sphere through women's sex-segregated institutions as a powerful feminist strategy. She argues that the failure of feminism was due in large part to feminists' attempts to integrate into the male world too early, right after suffrage was won. Hence, while O'Neill and Conway attribute the failure of feminism to an ideological defect, Freedman attributes it to the abandonment of a potent organizational strategy. Both Freedman and Blair agree that the woman's club movement made important contributions to the feminist movement, but Freedman sees these contributions in nonideological terms.

Freedman's admittedly speculative interpretation offers a valuable viewpoint from which to examine women's clubs. It is well grounded in cross-cultural comparisons that suggest the worth of a woman's public sphere.[52] Freedman's analysis is particularly promising because it offers a framework for the evaluation of women's clubs that frees us from excessive attention to ideas alone—without placing them in their structural setting. This is especially important given the lack of a straightforward connection between ideology and behavior.

Both O'Neill and Freedman interpret the woman's club movement within an analysis of the woman movement. A comprehensive discussion of the woman's club movement in this larger context is impossible here. But it is useful at least to compare the woman's club movement with the Woman's Christian Temperance Union (WCTU).

Like the GFWC, the WCTU was a mass organization of women—indeed, it was the first. The WCTU was organized in 1874. Under the direction of its charismatic leader, Frances Willard, the membership of the WCTU increased rapidly in the 1880s, when women were organizing women's clubs across the country. By 1890, when the GFWC held its first meeting, the WCTU had 150,000 members.[53]

The evolution of the activities of the GFWC and the WCTU involved a similar expansion of interests. Both began with respectable "causes." Like the

GFWC, the WCTU enticed its members into a variety of public activities in a wide range of fields. Both the WCTU and the GFWC had committees representing different areas of work. But the WCTU expanded its interests earlier than the club movement did; in the 1880s, Frances Willard developed the "Do Everything" policy, which encouraged WCTU members to become involved in whatever reforms they felt were most important. Hence, the WCTU and the GFWC used the same strategy to increase the public, indeed political, participation of women, the WCTU discovering this strategy earlier. Both gave the individual woman the freedom to find a path suited to her particular needs, to enter and remain in the public sphere.

And the WCTU, similar to the woman's club movement, drew heavily on traditional sex-role ideas to justify the expansion of women's activities. The WCTU based its appeal on protection of the home and family. Both the WCTU and the woman's club movement permitted women to participate in new activities, and develop a new sense of self, without demanding that they abandon strongly felt values about the family and the domestic sphere.[54]

Ruth Bordin has written a descriptive history of the WCTU in the nineteenth century. She emphasizes the mass appeal of the WCTU and its leading role in the woman movement during the 1880s and 1890s. She discusses at length the ways the WCTU used temperance to introduce women to political activity and how the WCTU permitted nonradical women to express feminist goals while maintaining a respectable cover. Bordin also describes the ways the program of the WCTU coupled nineteenth-century feminism with general reform. Bordin's book is a good description of the early history of the WCTU, but it frequently is marred by her attempts to demonstrate the WCTU was "better" than other contemporary women's organizations, especially the suffrage groups, women's clubs, and the GFWC. As Blair does with the woman's club movement, Bordin presents an optimistic analysis of the WCTU, with little discussion of its limitations.

Barbara Leslie Epstein explores some of those limitations in an analysis that is nevertheless quite sensitive and sympathetic to the WCTU. Epstein interprets the WCTU as part of a larger discussion of women's religious participation throughout the nineteenth century. She evaluates the WCTU in terms of the feminist impulse that supported it. According to Epstein, temperance was a women's issue because the temperance struggle expressed women's hostility to male culture and female subordination, and celebrated women's culture. Under the leadership of Frances Willard, the WCTU became a defender of women's interests. But in Epstein's eye, the WCTU fell short of being truly feminist; she calls it "protofeminist." Although the WCTU placed women's concerns at the center of its analysis, it could advance those concerns only within the framework of a male-dominated family structure. Epstein's argument is analogous to O'Neill's evaluation of social feminism. Both portray the limits of a feminist program that failed to challenge certain traditional assumptions about family organization and sex roles, and thus was held within the confines of patriarchal ideas.[55]

Organizations like the WCTU and women's clubs, and the woman movement generally, suggest that large numbers of women in the late nineteenth and early twentieth centuries were dissatisfied with a life confined to the home. Unable to abandon all the values and beliefs that confined them to that sphere, many women followed paths that permitted them to change their lives in ways compatible with apparently conflicting goals. The popularity of the woman's club movement indicates that it effectively addressed many women's needs, aspirations, and values; hence the club movement compels the attention of the historian of women. The concrete contributions women's clubs made to American urban life also make them important historically.

The work of Mary Beard and Estelle Freedman supplies the framework for my study of the woman's club movement in Wisconsin. In 1915, when Beard described the achievements of women in the public realm, she hinted at the larger implications of women's public, political participation. "Unknown women with large visions," she wrote, "form local associations. These local associations are federated into state and national associations." Beard looked to the development of a "conscious national womanhood" that would "soon disturb others than the village politicians."[56] Sixty years later, Freedman arrived at an analogous formulation, positing attempts to create a separate public sphere for women. Thus, even though Beard's chief concern was the value of women's work to the community, and Freedman's was the relationship of this work to feminist emancipation, both historians reach a similar conclusion.

This book asks questions of the Wisconsin Federation of Women's Clubs that are suggested by Beard and Freedman. What sort of public role did clubwomen seek to create for themselves, and with what methods did they attempt to increase their access to the public realm? What kinds of women became leaders in this setting? And how do people with no formal, acknowledged political voice operate in the public, political arena?

TWO

"Their Special Power Lies in Their Organization": The Wisconsin Federation of Women's Clubs

William Chafe has called the General Federation of Women's Clubs "a decisive voice in the Progressive Coalition."[1] At the state and local levels, too, clubwomen around the country supported many of the reforms of the Progressive movement. In this, Wisconsin clubwomen were particularly well-situated. Progressive leader Robert La Follette was from Wisconsin and was governor from 1902 to 1906, the time when Wisconsin clubwomen were constructing the machinery of their federation. This chapter expands on and qualifies points already discussed about the club movement generally. It describes how a women's organization successfully bound together members with casts of mind ranging from conservative to liberal. In such an organization, Wisconsin women formed alliances with many other contemporary reformers and created a public role for women who often considered themselves primarily "only" wives and mothers.

Lucy Morris, a clubwoman from Berlin, Wisconsin, was one of the driving forces in the formation of the Wisconsin Federation. In April of 1895, Morris became the General Federation's state chair of correspondence for Wisconsin. Women holding these positions in the GFWC represented the General Federation to the clubwomen of their state, serving as liaisons and encouraging clubwomen to participate in the GFWC. With the active support of Ellen Henrotin, then president of the GFWC, Morris formulated plans to organize a Wisconsin state federation.

Initially meeting apathy to the proposed federation among Wisconsin clubwomen, Morris organized a committee of a dozen leading clubwomen from throughout the state. Each member of this "correspondence committee" was assigned a district composed of several counties and was responsible for acquainting the clubs of her district with one another and encouraging them to share their ideas. In this way, Wisconsin clubwomen might experience firsthand the value of contact and cooperation.

After conferring with President Henrotin at the GFWC convention in May 1896, Morris and several of her supporters decided to launch the Wisconsin Federation. Correspondence committee member Lillian Mallory persuaded her well-known department club, the Milwaukee College Endowment Association, to host a meeting of Wisconsin clubwomen for the formation of the WFWC. Invitations were sent out in August and the meeting was held in Milwaukee in October. President Henrotin was on hand to encourage the delegates representing sixty-three Wisconsin clubs, who selected the highly respected Lucy Morris as the first president of the WFWC.[2] A year later, the Wisconsin Federation held the first of its annual autumn conventions. Each year, clubwomen of a different city hosted the convention and arranged convention programs, which included officers' reports; addresses and papers by other clubwomen and prominent "outsiders"; informal talks; and a variety of entertainments such as musical performances, literary readings, and purely social gatherings.

One of the first tasks of the WFWC was battling the apathy that Morris had encountered at the outset and convincing Wisconsin clubs to join the Wisconsin Federation. In 1896, the Federation's first membership directory listed 3,150 women, members of seventy clubs. By 1901, at the end of its first growth spurt, the WFWC had a membership of about 6,200 women and had more then doubled its original number of clubs. At this point, membership reached a plateau until 1905, when the Federation, with just over 6,350 members, began a period of slow but steady growth. By 1910, almost 7,350 women, representing 172 clubs, were Federation members. The slow growth in membership may have concerned Federation leaders; in 1910 they organized a publicity committee, which was replaced a year later by a club extension committee. Yearly membership tallies reveal another growth spurt beginning in 1910. By the autumn of 1917, several months after the United States entry into World War I, Federation membership included more than 13,500 women, members of 259 clubs.[3]

Despite some apathy from Wisconsin clubwomen, the Wisconsin Federation of Women's Clubs was launched in 1896 with the help of Lucy Morris. She became its first president that same year. (State Historical Society of Wisconsin.)

Like the GFWC, the Wisconsin Federation had standing committees whose number steadily grew during the first decades of the twentieth century. The development of WFWC committees is both a part of the Wisconsin Federation's history and a guide to the interests and activities of locally organized clubwomen in Wisconsin. (See Table 1 for chronology.) A particular standing committee usually emerged when some clubs had begun to do work in that field. Once formed, the committee then encouraged other WFWC clubs to take up the new work. Hence, the Wisconsin Federation's standing committees played a key role in fostering and channeling innovation within the WFWC and among its member clubs.

The Wisconsin Federation's earliest standing committees—education, library, and art interchange—reflected the educational and cultural concerns that first interested clubwomen.[4] From this beginning grew clubwomen's interests in institutions and legislation that affected community health and welfare.[5] Their appetites whetted by club study of history, clubwomen also undertook projects that preserved Wisconsin's past.[6] And they were among those who in the Progressive era first recognized the need to conserve natural resources.[7] Wisconsin clubwomen's broad sense of responsibility for human welfare, institutionalized in the standing committees, supported a wide and diverse range of work and activity.

Committees worked in several ways. To encourage Federation clubs to begin or continue work in the committee's area of interest, standing committees sent clubs letters and leaflets filled with information, suggestions for community projects, and practical advice. Frequently clubwomen's first step into a new activity was study of the relevant issues, so committees sent clubs bibliographies and study outlines, hoping that clubwomen would consult them when preparing club programs.[8] Committee reports at conventions described the year's activities of WFWC clubs, so delegates would return home with fresh ideas from the work of other clubs and with encouraging praise for their own.

Not always content with working solely through member clubs, the standing committees also initiated their own projects. The circular letters they sent to clubs sometimes requested money for committee projects, requests which met with varying degrees of success. The committees also actively supported legislation and other governmental action. Committee members attended and testified at legislative hearings, petitioned government officials and boards, and attempted to arouse and direct public opinion. They enlisted club aid and sent clubs letters asking, for example, that they inform local

TABLE 1

Chronology of WFWC Standing Committees[a]

Year Established	Name	Name Change
1896	Education	
1896	Library	1909: Reference Library
1897	Art Interchange	
1898	Town and Village Improvement	1907: Civics
1899	Consumers' League	1911: Industrial and Social Conditions
1901	Domestic Science	1904: Home Economics
1903	Landmarks	1914: Wisconsin History and Landmarks
1904	Loan Fund for Higher Education	
1904	Forestry	1911: Conservation
1904	Civil Service Reform[b]	
1908	Health	1911: Public Health
1909	Legislative	
1913	Music	
1914	Drama	
1915	Political Science[c]	1917: Woman Suffrage

[a]Excludes committees dealing with WFWC operations, such as the policy and club extension committees.

[b]Dropped in 1907; reorganized in 1911; dropped again in 1914.

[c]Subcommittee of the Education Committee.

legislators of their opinions on pending legislation.[9]

A closer look at the history of several committees reveals more clearly the roles of standing committees in the WFWC. By the turn of the century, some Wisconsin clubwomen had developed an interest in the problems of workers, especially women and children. At the 1899 WFWC convention, three clubwomen presented papers on "The Industrial Question as it relates to Women and Children." Florence Kelley, general secretary of the Consumers' League, attended this convention and described the work of her organization. The delegates responded by voting to establish a new Consumers' League standing committee, which was charged with cooperating with the National Consumers' League.

Over the years, the WFWC Consumers' League committee fought for state laws to protect workers and supported similar federal legislation. Via letters and talks at club meetings, it kept clubwomen informed of the work of the Consumers' League, modern industrial conditions, and the status of proposed legislation. The committee encouraged clubwomen to become actively involved by forming local consumers' leagues, surveying local working conditions, and reporting violations of the law to the authorities responsible for enforcement.[10] In 1911, it was renamed the Committee on Industrial and Social Conditions, reflecting the committee's broadened interest in a range of problems it associated with modern, industrial society, such as consumer protection, the spread of tuberculosis, and tenement conditions.

The success of this committee rested on the support of a group of WFWC leaders and a small but devoted nucleus of Wisconsin clubwomen. In 1907, WFWC president Martha Buell told convention delegates that the Federation's activities regarding the conditions of working women and children were the year's most important work.[11] But the Federation seems to have had mixed results in getting active, sustained concern from rank-and-file clubwomen. In 1911, Anna Manschot, the committee's chair, scolded clubwomen for their "apathy . . . in regard to social and industrial conditions."[12] Of course, few WFWC committees could claim that all clubs devoted significant time and energy to their particular areas of activity. But the Consumers' League committee may have had special difficulties, as the worlds of the factory and tenement were remote from the lives of most clubwomen, and the committee's subject matter was very political. Nevertheless, the committee's supporters kept the work for protective and other industry-related legislation alive and well among WFWC activities.

Unlike the industrial and social conditions committee, the domestic science committee, established in 1901 and later renamed the home economics committee, easily gained the widespread, active support of rank-and-file clubwomen. Interest in the newly emerging field of domestic science was evident at the earliest convention in 1897, where clubwomen reported establishing community home economics classes.[13]

Clubwomen offered several rationales for introducing home economics study in the schools. They reasoned that it would help improve the shortage of domestic help by providing a group of well-trained domestic workers. Since many clubwomen viewed household help as a necessity rather than a luxury, this justification struck a responsive chord. Furthermore, many clubwomen believed that recognition of home economics as an academic field would raise the status of their work as homemakers by demonstrating that household work required knowledge and expertise. Finally, clubwomen argued that the study of home economics by future homemakers would improve American family life, which would in turn improve social conditions.[14]

The domestic science committee arose out of an offer made by wealthy clubwoman Helen Kimberly, who was a strong supporter of the domestic science movement. In 1901 she offered the WFWC $5,000 for an educational loan fund if the Federation would raise twice that amount to endow a chair of domestic science at Milwaukee-Downer College, a Wisconsin school for women whose president, Ellen Sabin, served on the Federation's education committee. After lengthy discussion, the convention delegates accepted the offer. At the same time, they voted to petition the Board of Regents to establish a similar chair at the state university. Two years later, the legislature appropriated the necessary funds to teach domestic science at the university. And in 1904, the domestic science committee reported that the $10,000 had been raised through club and individual contributions, although with considerable difficulty.[15]

Although the domestic science committee was originally established to collect the funds for the chair at Milwaukee-Downer College, after completion of this project delegates voted to retain the committee. For years, this highly active committee promoted the introduction of home economics in Wisconsin's colleges and elementary, secondary, and normal schools. The committee also initiated projects to maintain and upgrade the standards of home economics study so that it would become an academically respected field.[16]

At first blush, an interest in home economics seems a step backward for women freshly entering the public sphere. But in fact it frequently was under the rubric of "home economics" that clubwomen left the realm of the private home. As early as 1901, when Lucy Morris prepared a study outline to accompany the Federation's traveling library on household economics, she included a section on "municipal housekeeping."[17] Clubwomen were told that caring for their homes and improving their towns and cities were essentially the same task, and that the former required the latter. When organized, the domestic science committee adopted this interpretation of "home economics." By 1916, the committee's report declared that "under 'home economics' falls the study of food, clothing, shelter, home management, and child welfare, with all their ramifications into the social, economic, legislative and health conditions of the community." Within a field of endeavor that they felt naturally belonged to them, traditional women could legitimately assert their interest in public activities that affected community welfare.[18]

Almost a decade after the establishment of the home economics committee, a health committee embarked on a course bound for similar enthusiastic support by clubwomen. The home economics committee paved the way by directing Wisconsin clubwomen's attention to the physical welfare of their families and the healthiness of their communities. By 1908, WFWC members and the civics committee were exploring ways clubs could combat tuberculosis.[19] Naturally enough, when the recently formed health committee reported to the 1909 convention, tuberculosis was its first major concern. It endorsed the work of the Anti-Tuberculosis Association, urging clubwomen to cooperate with its efforts.[20]

By 1911, members of the health committee had identified numerous public health measures worthy of support. The committee noted the passage of legislation it had endorsed, requiring the registration of nurses. The committee report discussed the value of similar registration of midwives; improved ventilation and sanitation in public buildings, especially schools; destruction of flies to control the spread of disease; sanitary food markets and pure food laws; and, community visiting nurses and medical examinations in schools.[21] Community health measures developed a prominent place in the club and Federation work of Wisconsin women.

In 1917, with its wide-ranging concerns and diverse program, the WFWC faced America's entry into World War I. When the combatants were limited to Europeans, Wisconsin clubwomen had passed resolutions urging United States and international efforts to obtain a peaceful settlement.[22] But when the

Ellen Sabin, a Wisconsin Federation of Women's Clubs member, was president of the Milwaukee-Downer College from 1895-1920. The Federation strongly advocated the academic study of Home Economics and in 1904 its education committee raised the funds to present an endowed chair in domestic science to Milwaukee-Downer College. (State Historical Society of Wisconsin.)

25

United States went to war, WFWC members' inclination to support the principles of peace was overcome by patriotic sentiments. With essentially no dissension entering its public records, the WFWC committed itself to civilian war work.

It received a warm reception from government and private agencies, which were calling on women to materially support the country's war efforts. A woman's committee was added to the Council of National Defense, which Congress had established to coordinate war work. This arrangement was mirrored at the state level. The Wisconsin legislature organized a Wisconsin Council of Defense with a woman's committee. Presidents of statewide women's organizations were members of this committee, including the president of the WFWC, Lettie Harvey.[23]

World War I was potentially a source of trouble for the Wisconsin Federation. Some women questioned the continued existence of the WFWC during a national emergency, fearing that women's time and resources might be diverted from civilian war work by Federation work. President Harvey defended the WFWC, arguing that "at such a time as this . . . organized strength is needed more than ever before."[24] Harvey and the women who worked with her kept the Wisconsin Federation alive by committing it to war service, and they guided its joint work with the Wisconsin Woman's Committee and the Red Cross. Through the WFWC and their local clubs, clubwomen participated in food conservation drives, war gardening, home and foreign relief work, Liberty Loan campaigns, knitting and sewing for soldiers, and preparation of surgical dressings. Already experienced in organized work, it was relatively simple for clubwomen to do organized war service, and according to Harvey, two-thirds of the women serving as heads of the countywide women's committees were clubwomen.[25]

But President Harvey and other WFWC leaders never lost sight of the Wisconsin Federation. At the 1917 convention, whose major theme was civilian war work, Harvey defined the importance of women's war contributions, but declared that this was not enough. She called on clubwomen to preserve and further Federation goals during the war, such as protecting child and female workers and maintaining clean streets, good education, and a pure food supply. "Is it not National Defense work Woman's Clubs have been doing in the past twenty-one years? Is it not patriotic to uphold, foster and improve our country's institutions?" she asked, appealing to clubwomen's belief that their club work was synonymous with defense of

During World War I Lettie Harvey defended the existence of women's clubs. As president of the Wisconsin Federation of Women's Clubs, she committed the organization to civilian war service, joining forces with the Wisconsin Women's Committee and the Red Cross. (State Historical Society of Wisconsin.)

American life.[26] Thus the WFWC survived the challenge of World War I, and a few years later the organization saw the enfranchisement of its members.

Standing committees were not the only organizational subunits of the Wisconsin Federation. Federation clubs were organized in just under a dozen districts, of several counties each, corresponding to Wisconsin's congressional districts. Each district was headed by a federation officer called a district vice president. By 1900, several districts had held annual district conventions, a practice that gained wide acceptability after the turn of the century. WFWC officers, especially the president and standing committee members, frequently attended these conventions. Clubwomen built increasingly elaborate district structures, and several districts became formal district auxiliaries or federations to the WFWC, with their own boards, committees, and officers. At times, there was some ill-feeling between district workers and higher Federation officers. Some WFWC leaders were jealous of the power of district officers and feared that the district federations might encroach on the state Federation's territory.[27] Sometimes Wisconsin clubwomen became confused over the place of the district auxiliaries within the framework of the WFWC, wondering how much autonomy district organizations possessed.[28]

Despite these problems, WFWC leaders generally encouraged the strengthening of district organizations, for it offered several advantages to the Federation. District work helped train clubwomen for higher WFWC positions. District conventions acquainted rank-and-file clubwomen who could not attend the annual convention with WFWC aims, methods, and leaders. The district vice presidents, acting as intermediaries between the Wisconsin Federation and the clubs of their districts, could mobilize clubwomen spread across a large state and organize the clubs for Federation work.[29]

The WFWC did not stand alone but was part of the larger national club movement. Supportive of its sister federations in other states, the WFWC also maintained numerous links to the General Federation. Early in its history, the WFWC joined the GFWC, which almost yearly sent officers to represent it at the Wisconsin Federation conventions. WFWC leaders likewise attended GFWC conventions and meetings. Frequently, the GFWC stimulated the WFWC to take up new projects and areas of concern.[30] But the General Federation was only one influence on the WFWC and by no means directed it. Many WFWC clubs did not belong to the General Federation, and many Wisconsin women had only a hazy understanding of its work, operation, and organization.[31] Thus, whereas Wisconsin Federation leaders were firmly committed to GFWC, the rank-and-file membership did not attach as much importance to it. And the WFWC certainly was never dependent on the General Federation for new ideas and expanded activities. Indeed, state federations sometimes influenced the GFWC to begin extensive work in new areas. There was a strong element of grassroots initiative in the club movement as a whole. Leaders could encourage, facilitate, and influence, but their ability to command was limited. Thus they usually required active support from the rank and file to get new work off the ground and keep it thriving.

Every organization faces difficulties attendant upon its structures, type of membership, and base of available resources. As hesitant as clubwomen were to complain, they often were forced to acknowledge these problems at conventions, as they searched for solutions. For example, the Wisconsin Federation was a statewide organization; its officers and committee members lived in all parts of the state. The board of officers, or a given committee, could not meet on short notice. Meetings had to be planned well in advance, and business often had to be conducted via the mail and, later, the telephone.[32]

Geography was one problem; another difficulty lay in the limited nature of Federation authority. Federation leaders could only suggest and guide, never compel. They were dependent on the willingness of clubs to do as they asked, and club cooperation was not always forthcoming. Frequently, WFWC leaders met with sheer club apathy—especially vexing in the slowness of answers to letters, if they were answered at all, and in club officers' failure to read circular letters to the full club membership.[33]

Difficulties also arose because Federation members generally had other significant responsibilities. Most had duties as homemakers, including some single women who cared for parents. Some had professional commitments; others maintained busy schedules with other organizations. Hence, one district vice president reproached standing committee members who refused invitations to the district convention because they could not "leave home," despite promises of assistance made in circular letters.[34] Members and leaders of the Federation varied widely in the time and energy they could, or would, give to it; some were genuinely overburdened. As is true in many volunteer organizations, Federation members did not always follow through.

But financial constraints were the most openly and frequently discussed of the Wisconsin Federation's recurrent problems. Annual dues paid by member clubs were the foundation of the WFWC treasury, which remained relatively small, never having a balance of much more than $400 in the first decade of the Wisconsin Federation's life.[35] Federation officers also found raising money for special projects difficult. A year after the WFWC began asking clubs for money for the proposed chair of domestic science, President Theodora Youmans upbraided clubwomen for not giving enough money despite their approval of the project. "When you give your voice, give your hand to help along. Moral support that doesn't do anything is not worth much." By 1904, one committee report noted that its work was limited by lack of funds.[36]

The Federation treasury grew slowly, reaching almost $700 in 1908. But ambitions grew more rapidly, and WFWC leaders found that lack of money severely limited their ability to act on their expanding interests. At the 1908 convention, President Martha Buell told delegates that "Until women have some financial independence, much of our work will suffer."[37] Treasurers' reports show that some well-to-do clubwomen had access to their own or their husbands' money and donated it to the Federation. But the average contribution of most clubwomen, for whatever reason, remained small.

Seeking financial independence for the Wisconsin Federation itself, in 1910 Federation leaders inaugurated a plan for a Federation Endowment Fund. They hoped to raise $10,000 and to use the interest from it to pay for Federation work, while leaving the principal intact. Perhaps in an effort to demonstrate to clubwomen the need for such a fund, committee reports began more frequently to describe the limits set by insufficient funds on Federation work.[38] But the contributions to the endowment fund came in slowly. A special finance committee, in reference to the endowment fund, said in disbelief and disgust, "in six years, ten thousand women have only raised about 4500 dollars. What is the trouble?"[39] Thus, in 1916 the newly elected president, Lettie Harvey, told clubwomen, "The Endowment Fund, like poverty, is still with us."[40] As ever, the Wisconsin Federation was dependent on club and individual contributions which were, for the most part, small, and was unable to compel anything larger. Relative poverty troubled the Wisconsin Federation throughout its first twenty-five years.

Nevertheless, the WFWC accomplished much. It helped its members participate in a variety of projects and causes and develop a voice in public matters. Surely not all, or even most clubwomen actively supported, or even cared about, all the Federation's areas of work. But at least some clubwomen supported each one. However, unlike most organizations, whose significance can be read largely in terms of the causes they supported and the programs they offered, the full meaning of the WFWC must be found elsewhere. The content of specific WFWC aims is only part of its story.

The theme of friendship among clubwomen, their emotional commitment to one another, recurs throughout the convention reports, from the first convention through World War I. No matter what business the Federation was attending to at the time, or what social problems were uppermost in clubwomen's minds, they affirmed in convention after convention their sense of companionship and affection. In her first presidential address, Lucy Morris saw this as one of the purposes of the Wisconsin Federation. "Am I not right in saying that . . . the spirit of loyalty of women to women . . . is being encouraged and manifested as never before in Wisconsin. That we are daily, yes hourly discovering the many noble, the many true, the many lovable qualities of our sister-women, and that larger sources of happiness are thereby opened unto us?"[41] Thereafter, Federation presidents frequently made such affirmations a part of their annual speeches, some even devoting major parts of their addresses to them.[42] Such feelings were generally expressed, too, at the opening of the conventions, in the addresses of welcome made by local clubwomen and Federation officers. Despite the almost ritual quality of these yearly declarations of WFWC camaraderie, and some officers' admonitions against petty snobbery and "exclusiveness," there is an underlying sincerity in these avowals of friendship.[43] Certainly, they were a crucial part of the Wisconsin Federation's self-image. And club work offered a basis for friendship different, perhaps, from the usual emotional experiences of many clubwomen. Vice President Jennie Aylward explained in 1915:

> One of the choicest compensations of club work are the friendships formed—often with people one could never know intimately in any other way. May I say that I believe they are different from those formed about the card table, over the teacups, or even those that come from reading and studying together? The friendships that come from working together for some common good have a quality all their own?[44]

The friendships that clubwomen enthusiastically celebrated were, of course, relationships among women. "We hear so much of the *brotherhood* of man. It is refreshing to know of the *sisterhood* of women," remarked President Mary Sawyer in 1905.[45] Wisconsin clubwomen were like clubwomen everywhere in that their consciousness of their sex was high. Many WFWC projects and proposals related to women. For instance, the educational loan fund made loans to women, and Federation leaders were particularly concerned with the conditions of the *woman* worker. The Wisconsin Federation called for a state reformatory for women like the one provided for men; it supported mothers' pensions to aid poor women with children. Members called for laws helping women whose husbands deserted them and giving women equal guardianship rights over their children.[46] While the Wisconsin Federation never claimed that the conditions of women were its sole or even chief concern, it did argue that clubwomen had a special responsibility to other women. Women of the WFWC did not address only practical problems of modern women's lives. They regularly discussed woman's nature and place in the world. Changes had taken place in women's lives in the past decades, and that they themselves were in the midst of such change. Lucy Morris, in her 1898 address, noted that "the kingdom of women has newly acquired territory," that social service, philanthropy, and education were now places of opportunity for women.[47] Almost fifteen years later, clubwoman Augusta Bolds made woman's changing position a major theme of her convention welcoming address. Once, she said, people had asked whether women had souls; later they questioned whether women could learn the alphabet. The nineteenth century witnessed the appearance of college-educated women, and now in the first decades of the twentieth century, women were closing in on the vote. Bolds continued: "But we marvel not less at the re-incarnation of the woman herself, newly clothed and equipped for twentieth century activities. *Yesterday in a faint at the sight of a spider, or in hysterics over a mouse, we can scarcely realize the evolutionary* process that has given us the athletic young woman of to-day, who with not the quiver of an eyelid can toss a burglar out a fourth story window."[48] Bolds' enthusiasm was not shared by all Federation women. Although they appreciated new opportunities for women, several WFWC presidents hastened to remark that clubwomen were not, and did not want to be, "new women."[49]

Wisconsin clubwomen were committed to many nineteenth-century notions about woman's place. They defined themselves, in role and temperament, as wives and mothers first, and in this way defended the concept of separate spheres. In 1897, Rose Swart, an Oshkosh educator and leading clubwoman, remarked that "the truly womanly is something different from the truly manly character."[50] Five years later, Ellen Sabin, a college president and WFWC leader, arguing for the teaching of home economics in schools, claimed that, "It is superfluous to train a girl away from the line she must follow. Home is woman's place, and home-making is the most womanly of occupations."[51]

Of course, as Karen Blair has demonstrated, clubwomen used such ideas to justify their public work. Rose Swart argued that because of her different character, woman belonged in public life, making the special contribution only she could make.[52] WFWC members reiterated such sentiments from convention to convention. "The time has come . . . when it is not enough that woman should be alone a homemaker, she must make the world itself a larger home," remarked President Ella Neville, as the new century began.[53] Fifteen years later, President Anne Kinsman indicated that little had changed in Wisconsin clubwomen's basic idea.

> The service we would render is the service of the home-maker. The enlarged duties of woman as home-maker, due to our changed industrial organization, challenge us to a broader service and a wider field of activity. Woman must be the home-maker in the community and in the state. Could one Federation have a more commendable mission than that of helping the guardians of the home to meet successfully their constantly enlarging task.

Kinsman went on to explain in these terms WFWC work in fighting tuberculosis, aiding poor children, improving education, promoting the causes of peace and equal suffrage, honoring the events and people of the past, and preserving Wisconsin resources.[54] The WFWC institutionalized this approach to woman's role in its home economics committee, which nurtured the clubwoman's sense of pride in her special place and womanly competence, and belief that caring for home and family required her public participation.

But this understanding of woman's role, and definition of herself as primarily wife and mother, did not prevent WFWC members from welcoming professional career women into their ranks. On the contrary, they supported these women as exemplifying women's distinctive and valuable public contribution. All that was needed was to characterize a given woman's profession in terms of peculiarly feminine abilities. For example, clubwomen argued that teachers were performing a service akin to the mother's task and were suited to their jobs because of women's child-rearing skills.[55] In return, professional women in the Wisconsin Federation paid homage to the importance of the homemaker's role.[56]

There are complexities and ambiguities attendant upon an ideology that endorsed woman's public participation on the basis of her private role and distinct feminine characteristics, the strategy Blair calls "domestic feminism." In several ways, a kind of defensiveness and an apologetic tone, traceable in part to the implications of this ideology, often crept into Wisconsin Federation discussions.

For example, clubwomen frequently reiterated that they were not deserting their special sphere because of their club work. Since they accepted the validity of assertions that women were uniquely responsible for the domestic realm, they had to show that club work was compatible with home responsibilities. They argued that women's clubs made women *better* wives and mothers. Even as late as 1915, Vice President Aylward noted that when clubwomen developed the "social consciousness" that impelled them to take up public work, they did not find "the hearthstone any less attractive."[57] Similarly, in 1908, President Buell assured convention delegates that although women might neglect some things in order to develop the more important aspects of club service, "there are certain things that we cannot neglect—our families, our home. These do not come within the pale of such consideration."[58] When club work conflicted with domestic life, Wisconsin Federation members were limited in their search for solutions to those which did not challenge woman's first responsibility to the home. For example, President Youmans encouraged WFWC delegates to support domestic science by threatening them with the spectre of "cooperative housekeeping schemes," which would be the only solution to the domestic servant "problem." The notion of cooperative housekeeping challenged the existence of private domestic realms presided over by individual women. Clubwomen could not acknowledge that cooperative approaches to housekeeping might free women from onerous domestic jobs because of their ideological commitment to the notion of separate spheres.[59]

WFWC members also hastened to reassure others—and themselves—that they had no quarrel with men. They emphasized that their aim was not conflict and competition, but cooperation. In 1897, Rose Swart argued that, "It is not as the rivals of men but as their loyal assistants that we should undertake public service."[60] Similarly, President Sawyer explained in 1905 that women's public participation should be "not in opposition to, but to supplement" that of men. "Thus may both work in harmony together. Man the guide; woman pre-eminently the *housekeeper* of the nation."[61]

Committed to a basic assumption of the status quo regarding the relationship of the sexes, women of the Wisconsin Federation found it difficult to acknowledge that their needs might conflict with men's. President Neville remarked in 1899 that Federation work taught clubwomen the unity of men's and women's interests. Some years later, President Sawyer asserted, "The men of America have ever been the champions of our sex."[62]

Avoiding conflict with men over the issue of gender, Wisconsin Federation women found criticizing men difficult. They took a conciliatory attitude toward male authorities and were timid about stepping on their toes.[63] When clubwomen did reproach men, they were forced to do so covertly, couching their criticisms in careful and complimentary terms. Said Swart, "Men are really wonderful beings. . . . They have made the world a good place to live in. This it becomes us to recognize and appreciate. But they haven't made it so good but it might be better."[64] Eight years later, President Sawyer was more specific about just what was wrong with things, pointing to "a spirit of greed that pervades the commercial world" and the "vigorous action of man" which was propelling the world at a dangerous rate. But she attributed these to men's "masterly activity, and God-given power of invention."[65]

Hence the Wisconsin Federation rarely articulated any sense of feminist grievance. That is, even though clubwomen would take pride in the changes that were occurring in women's lives and would celebrate women's advancement, they could not, at least in public, offer an analysis of what conditions limited woman as a sex. Some even blamed discrimination against women on women's individual characteristics, rather than on systematic societal prejudice.[66] They could admit that things were getting better for women, but they had trouble explaining what was wrong. Indeed, even when they argued that less fortunate women were the special concern of advantaged women, they quickly explained that their goal was the betterment of all humanity, not the improvement of their sex in particular. And generally, women of the Wisconsin Federation admitted not that they sought to increase women's power, but instead affirmed that they only wanted to increase women's contributions to the service of humanity. Denying that there was anything selfish about their motives, they claimed that their goals were altruistic.[67]

The defensive and careful tone of WFWC members regarding their public work varied from woman to woman. Some were forthright; others seemed more concerned with justifying their actions within a framework that left largely intact the notion of separate spheres. Variations are found with time, too; as the years progressed, Wisconsin clubwomen became more assertive and less apologetic.[68]

WFWC members' handling of the suffrage issue illustrates the intricacies of their notions about gender roles. Symbolically, woman suffrage represented the breakdown of the female private world, in distinction to the male public world. It signaled the entrance of women into the male preserve of that most public world—politics. When they first organized the WFWC, many clubwomen had relatively few qualms about working for or against certain specific laws. Asserting a general right to a voice in politics and legislative matters, however, was quite a different thing. Clubwomen's acquiescence to the notions of separate roles for men and women at first hindered their ability, as a group, to support women's political independence. But as they developed and acted on their ideas about gender, they were drawn into public participation, which over time lessened their resistance to woman suffrage.

In 1885, the Wisconsin legislature had passed a law granting women a limited suffrage—the right to vote on school matters. Hence, the first official mention of suffrage in the WFWC came from the education committee: in 1898, it urged clubwomen to exercise this limited right to vote.[69] As it turned out, a court had ruled that due to a technicality, this law was unenforceable. So in 1900, WFWC clubwomen established a temporary committee, which by 1902 obtained the necessary enabling legislation.[70]

The education committee, and WFWC officers, repeated from time to time their request that clubwomen vote on school-related questions. In 1902, President Youmans, who later became a leading Wisconsin suffragist, acknowledged the difficulty even this limited suffrage posed for clubwomen.

> Please do not feel that in voting on school matters you are committing yourself to any advanced suffrage theories or to the vicissitudes of a political life. . . . Your vote is simply an expression of your practical interest in the school, an interest that you have often expressed in other ways. As an abstract idea, voting indeed has its terrors, but when you remember that in this case your vote means simply a voice in the selection of the officers who direct the education of your children and in the settlement of other pertinent educational affairs, it seems only normal and rational.[71]

Youmans well recognized clubwomen's reluctance to admit to an interest in politics. When discussing the work of other state federations, she noted that some maintained standing legislative committees, "boldly proclaiming an interest and an intention that most clubwomen recognize, but that some think best to keep quiet about."[72]

But it became more and more difficult to maintain silence about such ambitions among clubwomen. In 1906 the Consumers' League committee urged clubwomen to consider the question of suffrage. As women's unquestionable responsibility for education made valid school suffrage, did not the need to protect working women and children justify suffrage?[73] Whether they liked it or not, clubwomen found themselves drawn into the world of legislative politics. Increasingly, convention delegates grappled with the impact of municipal, state, and even federal laws on their goals. In 1907, WFWC President Buell suggested that the Wisconsin Federation organize a legislative committee, as the General Federation and some other state federations had already done. That year, a Milwaukee clubwoman addressed the convention on "The Last Legislature: Our Gains and Losses," outlining legislative action on Wisconsin laws that were of interest to clubwomen.[74] In 1909, a legislative committee began reporting at conventions and lobbying for or against proposed Wisconsin laws. In its first convention report, the legislative committee justified its existence: "Many bills are introduced at every session of the legislature that affect the health, minds and morals of women and children. The merits and demerits of these bills are readily understood by women."[75]

Perhaps Wisconsin clubwomen were uneasy at the implications of it all. In 1910, President Carrie Edwards stated flatly, "The Wisconsin Federation of Women's Clubs is not political, not revolutionary."[76] A year later, even her more liberal successor, Emma Crosby, urged clubwomen to be cautious in their legislative work, to approach it with intelligent study, and avoid becoming the "prey of rival, political parties."[77]

Crosby's admonitions came with the belief that Wisconsin women would soon be granted full suffrage. A referendum granting Wisconsin women the vote was scheduled for 1912. At the 1911 Federation convention, delegates voted on requests from two Wisconsin suffrage organizations, both introduced by the same clubwoman, suffragist Jessie Jack Hooper. The Wisconsin Woman Suffrage Association asked the Federation to pass a resolution favoring woman suffrage, and the Political Equality League asked that suffrage be given a prominent place at the 1912 convention, which would be held shortly before the referendum vote. The 1911 delegates agreed "only" to encourage clubs to study the issue of suffrage and to ask the program committee for the 1912 convention to put it on the program.[78]

Amid much controversy, former-President Youmans introduced a resolution at the 1912 convention endorsing woman suffrage. But all resolutions had to go through the policy committee, the majority of which recommended that the WFWC *not* endorse woman suffrage. Youmans convinced the delegates to permit her to present a minority report, along with a telegram from Lucy Morris, who, unable to attend the convention, urged the assembled delegates to endorse woman suffrage. By a vote of 129 to 63, the delegates responded favorably to Morris's request.[79]

Wisconsin suffragists were greatly disappointed when the referendum failed by a wide margin. Despite the endorsement of suffrage, for several years afterward the WFWC was halfhearted in its practical, organizational support for the suffrage fight.[80] Perhaps Wisconsin Federation members feared

37

alienating their fellow clubwomen who still could not support suffrage. But individual clubwomen, including many WFWC leaders, did take an active part in the suffrage campaign.[81] Some WFWC members pursued a spirited drive to convince recalcitrant clubwomen that their place was in politics. The civics committee, for instance, "wished to emphasize that those who are interested in Civics are interested in Politics."[82] A year later, President Sophie Strathearn urged clubs to study political economy, noting that to improve things, clubwomen needed to understand governmental finances and politics. Thus, in 1915 the WFWC created the political science subcommittee that later became the woman suffrage committee.[83]

The logic of clubwomen's affirmation of a special, domestically rooted role for women initially kept many from supporting women's political independence. Yet that same ideology propelled them into activities that were nonetheless political. Thus, public, political participation lost the "terrors" of "an abstract idea" (to borrow Youmans's words); support for woman suffrage became a natural extension, for most clubwomen, of what they were already doing. In this sense, their ideology, their "domestic feminism," as Karen Blair calls it, was like a rubber band, which imposes restraints but stretches nevertheless. If she wanted to, a clubwoman could justify most things in the name of family, home, and children. And here may be an example of a complicated relationship between ideas and behavior; neither is *the* determining variable, but each impinges in turn upon the other.

The WFWC members' belief in the talents and abilities of women was crucial to this process.[84] They supported the public participation of women, convinced of the special and important contributions women had to make. This conviction underlay what historian Estelle Freedman called the woman's separate public sphere. Probably no clubwoman ever used just those words to explain what they were doing, but some came close. Addressing the convention in 1901, President Youmans marveled at the potential of the WFWC: "think of the power lying in the hands of these five thousand women who are fairly representative of the intelligent and progressive womanhood of the country, and who are thoroughly organized for work. Their special power lies in their organization, never lose sight of that."[85] Thus, Youmans and her Wisconsin Federation followers consciously sought to increase women's opportunities by maintaining an organization of women organized as women—what we might call a separate public sphere.

Beyond building their organization, members of the WFWC pursued several policies designed to ensure women's increased public participation. The

Woman's suffrage was not wholeheartedly endorsed by the Wisconsin Federation of Women's Clubs. At their 1911 convention, suffragist Jessie Jack Hooper introduced requests from two Wisconsin suffrage organizations to pass a resolution favoring the right to vote. The delegates agreed only to study the issue. (State Historical Society of Wisconsin.)

Wisconsin Federation and its member clubs sought, often successfully, to have women—*as women*—placed in public positions. For example, they wanted women on library and school boards; on boards of regents; on the State Board of Control of Penal, Charitable and Reform Institutions; and on the State Fair Board. They worked for female factory inspectors, policewomen, and female probation officers.[86]

Even though women holding such positions were participating in a male world, it is best to understand them in terms of the separate public sphere, situated firmly among female supporters. Having supported the appointment of women to particular positions, the WFWC maintained contact with them, for example, inviting them to address conventions and report on their work.[87] Although these women worked in the male public realm, they had a foundation in the world of organized women. In fact, sometimes clubwomen had a hand in creating their very jobs. By establishing libraries, clubwomen brought library boards into being. They supported efforts for changes in juvenile justice laws, which created the job of probation officer. They worked for improved government services and increased government responsibility, which brought the street and factory inspectors.

Furthermore, Wisconsin clubwomen expected that women like themselves would be chosen to fill these public positions. Frequently, clubwomen themselves were called on, a fact of which they were both conscious and proud. When they pressed for a woman factory inspector, a Milwaukee clubwoman was appointed. In committee and district reports, clubs reported on the appointment of one or more of their members to the library, school, or hospital board, or to the position of truant officer.[88] Clubwomen developed credentials through club work, and when government officials were convinced to appoint a woman, they turned to this readily available pool of talent. Indeed, since clubwomen were applying the pressure to appoint women, the choice of one of their own was most likely to satisfy them.

The WFWC increased the scope of the Wisconsin women's public sphere also by maintaining a network of connections with other organizations. Representatives of such organizations were invited to speak at Federation meetings, thus familiarizing clubwomen with their goals. Frequently, Federation delegates passed resolutions endorsing the work of other organizations and urging member clubs to promote their work in specified ways. In return, the Wisconsin Federation received invitations to the meetings of other societies. As the years passed, members of the WFWC became increasingly proud of these invitations and other requests for help; presidents began regularly disclosing to what meetings the Federation had sent representatives and which organizations had contacted the Federation for mutual aid. Convention programs included accounts of conferences and conventions attended by WFWC members. WFWC members often belonged to societies that the WFWC supported. Finally, such connections sometimes blossomed into projects in which the Wisconsin Federation collaborated with other organizations.

It is not at all surprising that the WFWC developed connections with other women's groups. Naturally interested in club work in other states, the Wisconsin Federation exchanged greeting and convention invitations with other state federations and frequently drew inspiration and new ideas from their work. But the WFWC went beyond this, maintaining connections with the Daughters of the American Revolution (DAR), the WCTU, the American Association of University Women, the National Congress of Mothers, and the Woman's Relief Corps (WRC).[89] It received information and requests for help from women's peace organizations, the National Council of Jewish Women, and Wisconsin suffrage organizations. Representatives of the Women's Auxiliary of the American Park and Outdoor Art Association addressed the Wisconsin conventions several times, tapping into WFWC members' interest in civic beautification.[90]

Leaders in the Wisconsin Federation acknowledged early the advantages of cooperation. In 1898, in conjunction with the Chippewa Falls Fair and the Wisconsin semicentennial celebration, the WFWC and other women's organizations, such as the WCTU and the WRC, collaborated on projects that gave them practical experience at cooperative endeavors. They also explored their differences and discovered their common grounds.[91] Over the years an eclectic organization like the WFWC found many mutual interests with other women's organizations. It exchanged ideas with the DAR regarding the preservation of Wisconsin landmarks; endorsed a temperance resolution presented by a clubwoman who was a county president of the WCTU; and turned its attention to literature, music, movies, and fair exhibits it found morally offensive after the National Council of Jewish Women requested help in its Purity of the Press campaign.[92]

Organizations of both sexes received as much interest from the WFWC. The WFWC's educational concerns led to connections with the Wisconsin's Teacher's Association. Connections with the Consumers' League were solidified in the Consumers' League committee. The Wisconsin Federation's strong support for the domestic science movement naturally resulted in links with the National Household Economics Association. When the Wisconsin Federation formalized its interest in landmarks preservation, it received enthusiastic support from the Wisconsin Archaeological Society, the State Historical Society, and county historical societies. And when the Wisconsin Federation developed an interest in public health, it began an extensive collaboration with the Wisconsin Anti-Tuberculosis Association. Other less-developed but real connections were formed with a range of organizations and associations—for example, the Drama League of America, the Red Cross, the American Play-Ground Association, the American Civic Association, and the National Pure Food Committee.[93]

And the WFWC sent representatives to all sorts of meetings, organized around specific social problems and attended by interested reformers from a variety of organizations and professions. Federation members were particularly attracted to state and national Conferences of Charities and Corrections, and congresses on peace, purity, and public health.[94] At this multitude of meetings, Federation members made contacts with other reformers and had the opportunity to exchange ideas.

While developing ties with organizations of private citizens, Wisconsin Federation leaders consciously sought to utilize government agencies. From its birth, the WFWC was closely allied with the Free Library Commission, and early suggestions from the town improvement committee noted the importance of cooperation with municipal authorities.[95] Concerned with community and self-education, WFWC members made extensive use of the Extension Division of the University of Wisconsin.[96] Soon, too, the WFWC turned its attentions to work with the Pure Food Commission, the State Forestry Commission, the Industrial Commission, and the Bureau of Child Welfare.[97] As the WFWC strongly and vocally supported the work of these agencies, their commissioners often found the attentions of the WFWC of practical value. The Pure Food Commissioner used clubs to promote his work by offering free of charge a pure food exhibit and speakers to clubs who would arrange some sort of pure food community event. Similarly, the Industrial Commission worked with the WFWC Committee on Industrial and Social Conditions to put together a pamphlet on women and children industrial workers.[98]

Thus, Wisconsin clubwomen gained access to the ideas and sometimes the structures of a variety of reform organizations. Having no specific, detailed program of its own, the Wisconsin Federation often acted as a clearinghouse for many progressive reform causes and special-interest associations. A woman interested in a given reform was provided with a group of women among whom she could recruit supporters. The "cause" of the WFWC during the first decades of the twentieth century was the public participation of women. Members could sojourn into the mixed or largely male world of official positions and private organizations. But they did so always with the backing of other women, with their feet planted in an organization of women who were held together by consciousness of their shared sex. Before they won the vote, Wisconsin women together found their public voice.

THREE

"To Agitate and to Educate": Wisconsin Federation Campaigns

At any time, the Wisconsin Federation of Women's Clubs was involved in a number of unrelated ventures. Among the diverse undertakings, some stand out as capturing more of the Federation's time, energy, and imagination. This chapter examines three WFWC campaigns, covering a period from the Wisconsin Federation's earliest years to a few years before the suffrage victory. It illustrates in more comprehensive detail the ways clubwomen gradually defined the terms of their public activity and political participation.

The Wisconsin Federation launched its first foray into the political arena at its very first convention in 1897, where Wisconsin clubwomen agreed to seek the appointment of two women to the State Board of Control of Reformatory, Charitable and Penal Institutions. The five members of this state bureau were responsible for inspecting a variety of state institutions and overseeing their operations.[1]

Inspection of community institutions by women already had some precedent. Their interest in education and the prerogatives they asserted as mothers—or potential mothers—led many clubs to organize school visiting committees, taking it upon themselves to visit local schools and make recommendations for improvements to school authorities. The practice of school visiting was one way that clubwomen, lacking official authority, created unofficial channels for influence.[2]

The Alexandrian Club of Sparta was one federated club that had visited local schools and reported its findings to the county superintendent. The president of this club, Mrs. G. H. Hall, served on the WFWC's education committee in 1897. Hall brought to the committee's attention deficiencies in the State School for Dependent Children at Sparta, an institution under the supervision of the Board of Control. The education committee made its own investigation and determined that the school's educational facilities were inadequate. In February of 1897, the committee sent letters to the governor and the State Board of Control, reminding them of "the especial obligation of the state in its relation of parent to the inmates of the school," and outlining ways to relieve the school's shortcomings. The committee was delighted to report at the convention in November that several of its recommendations were being implemented at the State School.[3]

With this success to back them up, the members of the education committee proposed a more grandiose plan: that the Wisconsin Federation convince the state legislature to pass a law adding two women members to the Board of Control.[4] This episode illustrates the tendency among clubwomen for small activities to mushroom into, and set precedents for, larger-scale activities. Clubwomen went from visiting the schools their children attended to visiting a state institution for children, and from there to requesting representation of women on the governmental body that oversaw a range of institutions. The education committee admitted to no incongruity in this progression, asserting its right to concern itself with any institution that housed, and presumably educated, children.[5]

The education committee offered several rationales for placing women on the Board of Control, all of them reflecting notions regarding women's special role, talents, and temperament. Turning women's disfranchisement into an advantage, the committee claimed that women, "unhampered by the restrictions of any political party," would be the perfect objective observers of state institutions. Stalwart housekeepers, they would be willing to closely inspect the beds and bathrooms of the institutions, "work which the male members of the Board would naturally shrink from doing." As natural domestic managers, women best understood how to maintain comfortable, efficient, thrifty homes. These skills, along with "the intuitive perceptions of women," would balance well with the "executive ability" of the male members of the Board. And, the education committee said, the women and girls in state institutions had some needs that were best met, perhaps only met, by women.[6]

Thus, even as they made this claim to public authority, clubwomen were asserting for women a duty to sit on the Board of Control because they were women, as opposed to a right to public power as politically equal individuals. Furthermore, in making its proposal, the education committee offered much in the way of deference to the men serving on the Board of Control. The committee thanked them for their "cordial . . . attitude" toward the education committee's suggestions and praised them as "honorable, high-minded men . . . [with] the best interests of each unfortunate member of every Institution of the State at heart."[7] Perhaps clubwomen needed to cushion with velvet their proposal that they lobby the legislature for women to be placed in positions of power.

The legislature would not reconvene until 1899, more than a year after the education committee made its proposal. In the meantime the committee kept busy. To demonstrate the value of having women on the Board of Control, the committee visited more than a dozen Wisconsin institutions and asylums. Again, reports from the education committee at the 1898 convention combined this assertive behavior with careful deference to male authority. The committee noted that prior to its visits, it explained its intentions to the Board of Control and obtained its approval. And it assured convention delegates that, "The Board of Control is doing a noble work and these visits were planned not in a spirit of criticism, but purely with a desire to note in what particulars a woman . . . could be of assistance on the board."[8]

The education committee reported that its visits were successful. It claimed to have obtained support from several superintendents of the institutions it visited for the appointment of women to the Board of Control. The committee concluded from its experience that the value of women in such positions was "self-evident." Again it appealed to reputedly feminine traits: "wise insight as regards to details," "the tenderness of the mother instinct," "innate delicacy" and "tender sympathy."[9] Invoking a domestic metaphor, the committee cited the complementary contributions of men and women that together maintained the family and asked why that arrangement would not be valuable in the management of state institutions as well. Thus the committee made clear that it intended neither to compete with men nor seize any of their power, but instead sought to have men and women collaborate in a mutual effort on the Board of Control.[10]

The committee also did not intend that just any women be given the opportunity to be of service. It went "on record as favoring the appointment of the *right woman only*. Much better no woman at all than the wrong woman." The appointed woman should have "tact," "ability, both natural and cultivated," and "familiarity with progressive educational methods." In short, the committee expected her to be a "true woman," with all the true woman's desirable and special characteristics.[11] In just these terms clubwomen described each other. In calling for the appointment of women to the Board of Control, the women of the WFWC were calling for the appointment of one of their own.[12]

Thus with a well-articulated, elaborate rationale based on traditional ideas, the committee staked out clubwomen's less than traditional claim to public authority. On February 15, 1899, Assembly Member Thomas McGrath introduced bill 227A, providing for the appointment of two women to the Board of Control as full, voting members.[13] The Federation's hand in the bill is evident in the residence of its sponsor. Both McGrath and the president of the Federation, Ella Neville, lived in Green Bay.[14] In the months that followed the bill's introduction, petitions from two federated clubs supporting the bill were entered into the Assembly's record, and the ninth district convention sent a similar letter to the Assembly.[15] According to Neville, "about twenty clubwomen" testified in favor of the bill at an Assembly committee hearing on February 23. Neville reported that the clubwomen "received the most considerate attention." Considerate or not, the Assembly committee gutted the bill, reducing the two full members to one auxiliary member who would have no vote in the Board's decisions. The bill was sent on to a second Assembly committee, which indefinitely postponed it.[16]

The extent to which the immature Wisconsin Federation waged a systematic campaign in support of the legislation once it was introduced is unclear; convention records do not suggest that such a campaign was mounted. At this early stage of its history, the WFWC probably was not yet well organized enough to mobilize its members in large numbers to place pressure on the legislature. The WFWC could call on its leaders, but at this point, its ability effectively to reach and motivate its widely scattered membership was probably limited.

Reporting the events surrounding the Board of Control bill, President Neville urged delegates to not lose faith. Having put in her good word for the assemblymen's kind treatment of testifying clubwomen, Neville argued that even if the WFWC lost this particular piece of legislation, it had helped increase public sentiment in favor of the proposal. She believed it ultimately would succeed.[17] Other clubwomen at the convention indicated they did not intend to forget the Board of Control episode. The education committee proclaimed that it had obtained the approval of the president of the Board of Control and would continue visiting state institutions "to be helpful with suggestions and advice until we are strong with power to act, with our two women on the Board of Control."[18]

Six years later, the WFWC witnessed Neville's promised success—at least in part. In 1905, Governor La Follette, who had connections with several club leaders, asked the Wisconsin legislature to pass legislation calling for the appointment of one woman to the Board of Control, and the bill was approved in June.[19] In 1917, a bill was introduced diminishing the status of the woman on the Board to auxiliary member and reducing her salary. Women's clubs sent petitions to the legislature against the proposed change, and the Federation appointed a special committee, headed by Lucy Morris, to lobby against the bill. The woman on the Board of Control retained her status as full member.[20]

The WFWC traveled a long road from its defeat in 1899 to its more self-assured, ready, and successful response in 1917. The first Board of Control episode called for action that was frankly political, still a problematic situation for many clubwomen at the close of the nineteenth century. Over time, clubwomen became more comfortable in the political realm. In 1907, the WFWC initiated a campaign against a proposed amendment to the state constitution. The WFWC brought to this task a more organized and well-developed machinery than it possessed in its earlier effort, and the cautious, defensive tone of the 1890s campaign was much less evident.

The proposed amendment that aroused the clubwomen's ire posed a threat to Wisconsin's kindergartens. From its first convention, the WFWC, like clubwomen across the country, supported an organized movement to introduce kindergartens throughout America's school systems. During the first ten years of the Wisconsin Federation's existence, member clubs reported their own work efforts to start kindergartens in their communities or convince local school authorities to do so. The education committee frequently reiterated its interest in the promotion of kindergartens, and convention delegates often heard addresses on the accomplishments of kindergartens.[21] Any law that jeopardized the clubwomen's promotion of kindergartens risked the opposition of the WFWC.

In January 1907, Wisconsin Assemblyman Roderick Ainsworth introduced a bill to change Article X, Section 3 of the Wisconsin Constitution, which required the maintenance of free public school open to all children between four and twenty years old. Money from the state's school fund was disbursed to school districts according to each district's population between these ages.[22] The Ainsworth Amendment raised the lower limit from four years to six years. During the first half of 1907, Ainsworth's bill made it through the round of Senate and Assembly hearings to approval by the full legislature in June.[23]

Ainsworth maintained that it was disadvantageous to allow children under six years into the regular school, asserting that they could not do the work required and that they disrupted the work of older children. He claimed to be a supporter of kindergartens and asserted that his proposal still permitted communities to establish special kindergarten facilities and so was no threat to the kindergarten movement. But many educational authorities and legal experts disagreed. Some felt that the effect of his amendment would be the prohibition of kindergartens. Others argued that at the very least the Ainsworth Amendment seriously threatened the financing of kindergartens because it cut off regular state funds for them, forcing communities to agree to a special levy if they wanted to maintain kindergarten facilities.[24]

For the Ainsworth Amendment to become part of the Wisconsin Constitution, it would have to pass the next session of the legislature, due to convene in 1909, and then be ratified by the voters. So in June 1907, opponents of the measure had time to wage a fight.

A Milwaukee clubwoman, Gertrude Cushing, brought the amendment to the attention of the WFWC at the convention in October 1907. Cushing was a leader of the Social Economics Club and a member of the Milwaukee College Endowment Association (both federated clubs). She also had served as a district vice president from 1904 to 1906. At the 1907 convention Cushing presented a report called "The Last Legislature: Our Gains and Losses," in which she discussed the Ainsworth Amendment. She explained the threat it posed to kindergartens and the process by which it could become law. Cushing then outlined a sophisticated plan of attack against the amendment, based on dissemination of information, grassroots organizing, and pressure on the legislature. Cushing's plan exploited the strengths that had been built into the WFWC's district organization; she made district officers especially responsible for supplying the clubs of their districts with information and coordinating their activities against the amendment.[25]

Cushing also called on clubwomen to become seriously involved in the political process. She asked them to canvass their districts systematically prior to the primary and make each candidate aware of the reasons for opposing the bill. Cushing directed that those representatives returning to the legislature who had previously voted for the Ainsworth Amendment be "convinced of the error of their ways, by moral suasion when possible or if necessary with a club always using the most influential club in the district for that purpose." Finally, Cushing suggested that an afternoon at the 1908 convention be devoted to a discussion of the Ainsworth Amendment.[26]

The WFWC accepted Cushing's report and set about implementing her plan. A special committee composed of the district vice president and chair of the education committee worked with the education committee to raise the awareness of clubwomen and the public regarding the problems posed by the Ainsworth Amendment.[27] By March of 1908, only six months after the 1907 convention, Wisconsin newspapers credited the WFWC and women's clubs with active, effective opposition to the Ainsworth Amendment.[28] District vice presidents reported keeping the issue in view on their terrain; district conventions were especially helpful in mobilizing public opinion against the amendment. In October 1908, the Milwaukee Social Economics Club distributed thirty thousand leaflets against the amendment, and many other clubs both large and small reported agitating against Ainsworth's proposal.[29]

The WFWC convention in October of 1908 attracted much attention because its program included an afternoon of debate among Ainsworth, supporters of the kindergarten movement, and legal experts who disagreed with Ainsworth's assessments of the effects his amendment would have. The *Milwaukee Journal* headlined its account of the debate, "Women or Men Win; State Women's Club Meeting Has Lively Time Over the Kindergarten."[30]

The WFWC did not rely solely on its own organizations to defeat the amendment, but also drew on its connections and good relations with Wisconsin educators and their organization, the Wisconsin Teachers Association (WTA). The 1907 WTA convention was held a few weeks after the WFWC convention. At the WTA convention, Carrie Morgan, the superintendent of schools in Appleton and a clubwoman who had served four years on the Federation's education committee, presented a paper entitled "What Women's Clubs Can Do For Kindergartens." The convention also established a committee of five to investigate the Ainsworth Amendment and recommend a course of action regarding the proposal to the WTA.[31]

Like the 1908 WFWC convention, the teachers' convention of 1908 pitted Representative Ainsworth in a debate against kindergarten supporters. Clubwomen attended the WTA convention, and one of Ainsworth's chief opponents in the debate was Cushing, who had been invited to present the initial case against the amendment. During the course of her presentation, Cushing asked the WTA to throw its weight against the bill.[32]

51

Cushing got little argument from the WTA. The WTA special committee recommended that the convention oppose Ainsworth's bill. The special committee's cordial relationship with Wisconsin's woman's club movement was evident in the committee's report, which credited the WFWC and its clubs with considerable effort against the amendment. The committee remarked:

> The significance of this action by many bodies of intelligent women in the state becomes apparent when we remember that in most cases the establishment of the kindergarten in any community has been due to the active and persistent efforts of the women in that community. The position of these women who have been most ardent advocates of the kindergarten and most thorough students of its principles and the results of its work should have very great weight in the discussion of the question as to whether the kindergarten shall be retained as a part of the public school system.[33]

Voices raised in opposition to Ainsworth's proposal continued to multiply. By November of 1908, newspapers throughout the state were generally opposing the amendment, once aroused into expressing an opinion by the publicity campaign waged against it. When the legislature convened in 1909, Wisconsin school boards had joined the opposition to the Ainsworth Amendment.[34]

The Ainsworth Amendment died; it was not reintroduced into the Wisconsin legislature. Clubwomen at the annual convention in October 1909 congratulated themselves for the "stormy season" they had created for the amendment.[35] A week later at the WTA convention, Nina Vandewalker, a leader in the kindergarten movement, attributed the defeat of Ainsworth's proposal to the joint efforts of the WFWC and Wisconsin educators.[36] It is worth noting the lead role the Federation took, announcing its opposition to the amendment a year before the WTA.

The campaign against the Ainsworth Amendment demonstrated to Wisconsin Federation members, if there were any doubters, the efficacy of their sometimes elaborate organizational machinery and the value of collaboration with other, perhaps more powerful, organizations. It also strengthened the position of clubwomen who believed that the Wisconsin Federation had a legitimate place in the political process. The danger that the Ainsworth Amendment posed to kindergartens, to which clubwomen had devoted significant energy, was enough to override many clubwomen's abstract misgivings about their political participation. Genevieve Colemen, chair of the Federation's special committee on the Ainsworth Amendment, acknowledged and dismissed these qualms when she described the work of her committee: "One woman said: 'Working just like politicians,' whatever that may mean."[37]

At least some clubwomen were aware that without the vote their place in the campaign against the amendment was difficult; they could not back up their opposition to the legislation with a threat to vote against representatives who supported it. In setting forth her plan, Cushing said she hoped that if the plan were carried out "the results may prove that although we have not been granted a franchise, we are able to make or unmake the laws."[38] At the 1908 convention, one delegate wondered whether, since it involved a school question, women might participate in a vote on the amendment if it passed the 1909 legislature. She was told that the limited school suffrage women possessed did not extend to constitutional questions.[39]

But the delegates at the 1908 convention heard more about their political power than their weakness. Remarked the special committee on the amendment:

> The twelve women forming this committee, with malice toward none and charity for all, feel impelled to assert that the law makers of Wisconsin are going to have a hard time of it next winter, unless they agree with the women on the kindergarten question. And this recalls that a noted English physician once said "In America the woman governs the man absolutely. In a sense, the last man that came to America was Christopher Columbus." If this be true, here then is a golden opportunity. To agitate and to educate form a combination of strong power.[40]

The campaign against the Ainsworth Amendment was one giant step on the WFWC's journey toward fuller political participation. The Wisconsin Federation's first standing legislative committee was appointed at the 1908 convention, with Cushing at its head.[41] A year later, in its report to the 1909 convention, the legislative committee described its first lesson: Special-interest lobbies frequently used less than honorable means to pass or defeat legislation. Sounding a conciliatory note, the committee remarked that it was not "[impugning] the motives of legislators," but then castigated them for "ill-considered, ill-drafted bills," failure to "understand conditions," and "shockingly mismanaged official housekeeping."[42] More than ever before, after playing their role in the defeat of the Ainsworth Amendment, WFWC members were ready both to criticize deficiencies in the male world of politics and to enter that realm in defense of their concerns. Three years later, in 1912, the Wisconsin Federation endorsed full suffrage for women.

No doubt many members never felt fully comfortable with the WFWC's expanding role in political matters. As nonvoters, they had learned that they could make a significant impact on the public world by disseminating information to reshape public awareness and mold public opinion.[43] In 1916, Wisconsin clubwomen participated in a national "Baby Week" celebration, whose goal was the reduction of infant and maternal mortality. The organizers of Baby Week hoped to make available information on proper care of babies and new mothers. They believed that if people knew that infant and maternal mortality were at least partially under human control they would demand appropriate health measures from physicians and government.[44]

The proposal for a national Baby Week was jointly formulated by the General Federation of Women's Clubs and the United States Children's Bureau, headed by Julia Lathrop.[45] The triple association of organized women, concern over infant mortality, and the Children's Bureau originated well before the 1916 Baby Week celebration. Some years before the Bureau was established, clubwomen throughout the United States had campaigned for improved birth registration, which was considered vital in the reduction of infant mortality: without it, isolating the factors involved in infant deaths was impossible.[46] Women's organizations had lobbied for the creation of the Children's Bureau, and subsequently groups including the GFWC, the Mothers' Congress, and the Association of Collegiate Alumnae had collaborated with the Bureau on some of its projects.[47] Among the Bureau's first important activities were detailed studies of infant mortality, publication of popular pamphlets on prenatal and infant care, and continued efforts to improve birth registration.

This work and previous baby-saving celebrations organized by women in cities across the country culminated in the plan for a nationwide Baby Week.[48] Acting in collaboration, the GFWC and the Children's Bureau provided the initial publicity to obtain the cooperation of local clubwomen. Drawing on the experience from locally organized baby-saving celebrations, the Bureau and the GFWC made available information on how to organize a successful Baby Week.

The GFWC mailed appeals for cooperation to its members and channeled appeals through state federations.[49] In 1915, GFWC President Anna J. H. Pennybacker attended the Wisconsin Federation's annual convention, requesting Wisconsin clubwomen's participation.[50] Pennybacker made her appeal to an interested, well-primed audience. Public health measures already were high on the agenda of clubwomen, and many of their public health efforts related directly to the well-being of children and their mothers. One of the most ambitious of these was the Infant's Fresh Air Pavilion, operated by the Milwaukee Woman's Fortnightly Club, where poor mothers could bring their babies for basic medical care and advice. Convention speeches addressed the problems of infant health; committees urged clubwomen to work for visiting nurses and medical examinations in schools. In 1911, the WFWC sent a message to Wisconsin's congressional delegation asking that they support establishment of the Children's Bureau. Convention delegates passed relevant resolutions, including one that recognized the connection between childhood and later adult health and called for specific measures to protect children's health, and another that encouraged clubwomen to assist the state Bureau of Child Welfare in obtaining a rural nurse who would concentrate on prenatal care.[51]

Communities throughout Wisconsin responded to the call to celebrate Baby Week. Of the eighty-three communities that reported celebrations in 1916 to the Children's Bureau, more than four-fifths had clubs that belonged to the WFWC. Clubs sponsoring Baby Week celebrations combined education with entertainment as they had been doing for years at club meetings and other community events.[52] In addition to lectures and demonstrations on prenatal and baby care by medical experts, public health authorities, and clubwomen, programs included special exhibits, store displays, literature distribution, plays on health-related themes, and baby contests.[53]

The WFWC played a significant part in Wisconsin's Baby Week campaign, well beyond the role of passive conduit for the plans of the GFWC. WFWC leaders made it easier for local clubwomen to assume the work of sponsoring a Baby Week. They gleaned information from a variety of sources on infant and maternal health and on baby-saving celebrations, making it available to clubwomen throughout the state.[54] Federation leaders suggested potential Baby Week projects, and at the 1915 convention offered a timetable for clubwomen to follow to ensure that they had sufficient time to arrange events.[55] The WFWC committed its organization's machinery to promotion of the campaign, using its officers, committees, district leaders, and between-convention meetings to keep Baby Week plans on track. The WFWC committees on public health, civics, and home economics were jointly responsible for much of the work.[56] And WFWC President Anna Kinsman urged "interested women" in communities without federated clubs to arrange local Baby Weeks.[57]

Perhaps the greatest asset Wisconsin clubwomen brought to Baby Week was their ability to mobilize and coordinate the participation of a range of organizations and people in a community effort. For the Baby Week observance, the Wisconsin Federation was well served by its extensive connections with other state organizations, institutions, and government agencies. In 1915, President Kinsman made a variety of appeals for help, obtaining positive responses from the Wisconsin Anti-Tuberculosis Association, the Free Library Commission, the Extension Department of the University of Wisconsin, and the State Board of Health. These groups helped supply the arsenal of advice, literature, and speakers the WFWC made available to its clubs.[58] At the local level, too, where the clubs of a city or town often jointly sponsored the event, clubwomen made their Baby Weeks a success by obtaining the cooperation of the community's doctors, nurses, ministers, teachers, librarians, editors, business owners, and government officials.[59]

WFWC leaders were particularly proud of the cooperative aspect of Baby Week observances.[60] Over the years, the WFWC had learned how to tap into the resources of other organizations and institutions, and Federation leaders saw in the Baby Week campaign the results of their efforts to maintain these connections. The Children's Bureau report on the 1916 Baby Week singled out Wisconsin clubwomen for their success in coordinating the work of several state agencies.[61]

The results of the 1916 Baby Week campaign are difficult to measure, but it is certain that it had effects beyond that year's celebration. Encouraged by the public's attendance,[62] clubwomen organized another Baby Week in 1917. WFWC President Lettie Harvey noted that although civilian war work competed for clubwomen's time and resources, many clubs put together some sort of observance.[63] In 1918, the Children's Bureau, with the cooperation of the Woman's Committee of the Council of National Defense, launched an even more ambitious Children's Year Campaign. The culmination of previous Baby Weeks, this year-long campaign expanded the focus from the well-being of babies to the health, recreational, and educational needs of all children.[64]

The leaders in the Baby Week campaign of 1916 hoped for more results than another celebration a year later. In reviewing for convention delegates the 1916 campaign, WFWC leaders stressed the importance of follow-up work to institute measures like visiting and rural nurses, better birth registration, and free clinics for poor mothers and their babies.[65] And many Wisconsin clubs did follow through on the 1916 Baby Week effort, starting anew or reinvigorating public health activities.[66]

Finally, the participation of clubwomen in Baby Week may well have contributed to the passage of the Sheppard-Towner Act in 1921. The act created the first health program financed by the federal government, providing for the establishment of health clinics to reduce maternal and infant mortality. Like the Baby Week observances, these clinics focused on dissemination of information to prevent illness and ensure health. In 1917, Julia Lathrop had proposed a forerunner of Sheppard-Towner. When woman suffrage finally came in 1921, politicians searched for ways to win the allegiance of the new female voters. To satisfy the newly enfranchised women reformers, congressmen voted for the Sheppard-Towner Act.[67] In their work of the prior decade, and most recently and memorably in their Baby Week campaigns, American women had demonstrated the priority they placed on promoting maternal and infant health. And national and state women's organizations lobbied for the passage of Sheppard-Towner.[68]

Still, even without the vote, the WFWC found ways in its first twenty-five years to attain power in the public arena. As the WFWC multiplied and strengthened its structures—its districts and committees—the WFWC created a machine that could apply continual pressure to mobilize even hesitant, inertia-ridden clubwomen. By participating in a network of volunteer organizations, government agencies, and Wisconsin institutions, the WFWC allied itself with those having power and resources that clubwomen often did not possess themselves. Initially somewhat cautious and defensive, as in the Board of Control episode, two decades later the Wisconsin Federation had developed enough self-assurance to direct its state's efforts in a nationwide campaign planned and sponsored largely by women.

FOUR

"Mothers of the Federation"

The Wisconsin Federation of Women's Clubs took pride in its efforts to unite women from all parts of the state. Like its members generally, the Wisconsin Federation's leaders came from towns and cities in most regions of Wisconsin. Who were these women who guided the Federation? What sorts of experiences and talents did they bring to WFWC? What kind of women did Wisconsin clubwomen choose to follow?

This study of WFWC leaders is based on sixty-six women, who, between 1895 and 1920, made a substantial commitment to the Wisconsin Federation. The time Federation members spent in WFWC leadership roles, and the nature of those roles, served as the criteria that measured "commitment." The sample includes three categories of women: those who held a Federation-wide office (president, vice president, secretary, treasurer, or auditor) for a two-year term and served two or more years in any other WFWC capacity; those whose highest office was district vice president and whose total WFWC service lasted five years; and those who served only on committees, but did so for at least eight years. A variety of sources provided information about these women: obituaries; county and local histories; WFWC convention reports; biographical dictionaries; histories of Wisconsin women; records of organizations; manuscript collections; city directories; the census; and the magazine *Wisconsin Clubwoman*. The limitations of the sources affect the kinds of conclusions that may be drawn. Gaps in the data are especially significant. I found almost no information for about twenty of the sixty-six women. Thus, the data are best used to make positive statements regarding these women. For example, the statement that fourteen WFWC leaders belonged to the Wisconsin Women Suffrage Association does not mean that fifty-two did not belong. It means that *at least* fourteen WFWC leaders also were members of the WWSA. I found census information for almost all of these women.

Obituaries, one of the most valuable sources, were located for forty-one of the women. The obituaries varied greatly in thoroughness and detail, a few providing almost no useful information.[1]

Despite the limitations of missing data, the sources yielded enough information to draw significant conclusions about WFWC leaders. The ready availability of census data provides a fairly complete, basic demographic portrait of these women. The majority of WFWC leaders were married; almost 15 percent were single. As a group, WFWC leaders were comparable in marital status to other native-born, white Wisconsin women (see Table 2).

TABLE 2

Marital Status

	WFWC Leaders		Wisconsin Women[a]
	number	percent	percent
Married	56	84.8	73.3
Widowed	1	1.5	8.6
Single	9	13.6	17.1

[a]Based on figures for native-born white women twenty-five years and older, which of the available data best matched the age and ethnicity of WFWC leaders. [Source: U.S. Bureau of the Census, *Thirteenth Census of the United States: 1910. Abstract with Supplement for Wisconsin*, p. 597.]

Most married Federation leaders had children, but they had far fewer than did Wisconsin women generally (see Table 3). On the average, married WFWC leaders had 2.5 children.

TABLE 3

Fertility of Ever Married Women
(By Birth Year of Woman)

Woman Born:[a]	Average No. of Children Born to White Wisconsin Women	Average No. of Children Born to WFWC Leaders	No. of WFWC Leaders[b]
1836-1860	5.46	2.87	30
1861-1865	4.69	2.00	10
1866-1890	3.28	1.85	13

[a]These categories cover uneven time spans reflecting the way data were reported in the census. [Source: U.S. Bureau of the Census, *Sixteenth Census of the United States: 1940. Population. Differential Fertility, 1940 and 1910: Fertility for States and Large Cities*, pp. 142, 160.]

[b]Number of children was not known for four leaders, so these figures do not add up to 57.

Such smaller than average families may be a reflection of the social class of Wisconsin Federation leaders. But even if this is the case, it suggests that leaders' family responsibilities were less demanding, in quantitative terms, than those of their contemporaries. Furthermore, over half of the women in the leadership group had live-in domestic servants, according to the 1900 or Wisconsin 1905 census (or both). On the other hand, their ideological commitment to the primacy of home and family duties may have made their domestic responsibilities more onerous and time consuming than their small families would suggest.

This potentially complex interaction between domestic duties and club work is illustrated by the place of club work within the life cycle of WFWC leaders. The average age of Federation leaders when they assumed their first Wisconsin Federation post was forty-five years. (Their club work began at least a few years before that.) This holds for all these women, whether their numbers are broken down as single women, married women, or women with children. Twenty-five years was the earliest age at which a WFWC leader assumed her first Federation office, sixty-two the latest.

The information indicates that participation in a local club was compatible with caring for young children, at least for WFWC leaders (see Table 4). More than a quarter of them managed it, and several continued club work throughout one or more pregnancies. But responsibility for young children may have been more difficult to combine with Federation duties, taken on always in addition to local club work. Only one-sixth of the women in the leadership sample had children six years or younger when they accepted their first WFWC position, and they usually had only one young child.

As their children got older, women were more likely to hold WFWC offices. This probably reflected the difficulties women faced in coordinating the demands of child care and organizational leadership. It also may have been a by-product of women's preference for the leadership of middle-aged and older women. Whichever is the case, Table 4 indicates that Federation leaders were at a range of stages in their life cycles when they began their WFWC service, although they were not at the height of the child-bearing and child-rearing cycle. Some leaders at some times may have experienced conflict between Wisconsin Federation work and domestic responsibilities. But there always was a group of leaders unlikely to be seriously hindered solely by family duties. Individual difficulties in specific cases certainly arose, but the WFWC was unlikely to have foundered on its leaders' commitments to their own domestic spheres.

The leaders of the WFWC were fairly uniform in their class background. Not surprisingly, they represented mostly the middle, upper-middle, and upper parts of the social strata. One valuable indicator of their class is their husbands' occupations. As Table 5 demonstrates, of the fifty-four married women for whom such information was found (the widow is not included here), four-fifths of their husbands had substantial businesses or professional occupations. Of the businessmen, about half were highly successful, prominent, even wealthy. These men had multiple business interests, which included lumber, timber, mining, railroads, real estate, paper manufacture, and banking. For

TABLE 4

Club Work and Child Care Responsibilities

	Number of Leaders	Percent of Total Sample of Leaders
Club Work: youngest child six years or younger	19	28.8
Federation Work: youngest child six years or younger	11	16.7
Federation Work: youngest child seven to thirteen years	12	18.2
Federation Work: youngest child thirteen to eighteen years	10	15.2

example, Helen Kimberly's husband made a "huge fortune" in paper manufacturing by founding Kimberly-Clark Corporation. Thomas Bardon, husband of Jennie Bardon, was the president of mining companies and of Ashland National Bank, and also had financial interests in a timber company. Carrie Edwards's husband had lumbering interests in Wisconsin, Idaho, Arkansas, and California. Eleven Federation husbands also had significant public careers, as mayors, legislators, and attorneys generals.

What of the unmarried women? Of these ten women (the widow is included here), six are known to have had paid occupations. Although as women they faced wage discrimination, their jobs were professional ones. Five were educators, ranging from a college home economics instructor to the president of Milwaukee-Downer College. The sixth was a librarian and library organizer, and later a lecturer and writer.

TABLE 5

Husbands' Occupations

Occupation of Husband	Number of WFWC Leaders
Prominent businessman[a]	10
Businessman	9
Banker	4
Lawyer	10
Physician	4
Educator[b]	3
Newspaper owner/editor	2
Architect	1
Other[c]	11
Unknown	2

[a]Prominent businessmen owned large businesses and generally had interests in several business ventures. Businessman had smaller, more community-based interests, for example, a drugstore or a pen manufacturing company.

[b]Includes a professor of economics, a high school principal, and a president of several educational institutions.

[c]Includes a boat builder, train dispatcher, train engineer, farmer, accountant, bank cashier, and several salesmen and insurance agents.

The religious affiliations of these women also suggest that WFWC leaders came from the middle and upper social classes (see Table 6).

TABLE 6

Religion

Religion	Wisconsin Religious Population (percent)[a]	WFWC Leaders (percent)[b]	WFWC Leaders (numbers)
Congregationalist	2.6	47.4	18
Presbyterian	1.8	21.1	8
Episcopalian	1.7	13.2	5
Methodist	5.5	7.9	3
Catholic	50.5	5.3	2
Unitarian/ Universalist	unavailable	5.3	2
Lutheran	27.9	0	0

[a]Based on Wisconsin residents with a religious affiliation, 1906. Not all Wisconsin denominations are reported here. [Source: U.S. Bureau of the Census, *Religious Bodies: 1906*, Part 1, pp. 371-72.]

[b]Based on number of cases where religious affiliation is known: thirty-eight.

Congregationalists were best represented, followed by the Presbyterians and Episcopalians. These three Protestant denominations, representing the religious roots of America's colonial settlers, account for more than three-quarters of the WFWC leaders whose religion is known. This contrasts sharply with Wisconsin's religious population generally, which was dominated by Catholics and Lutherans, reflecting the German, Scandinavian, and Eastern European immigrants who settled there throughout the second half of the nineteenth century. Hence, the available information demonstrates that WFWC leaders were largely members of Wisconsin's middle and upper classes.

To a somewhat lesser extent, Wisconsin Federation leaders had several other significant life experiences in common. For example, WFWC leaders comprised a strikingly well-educated group of women (see Table 7). More than seven times as many of these women attended college and normal school than did their contemporaries; at least 33.3% of WFWC leaders attended college or normal school for at least a year, compared to only 4.6% of Wisconsin women born by 1885 (as were all of the women in the leadership sample). [2] Others did special study of art or music; a few had graduate or professional training. Information on the education of WFWC leaders is incomplete, so it is probable that these figures underestimate the educational level of these women. The potential for intellectual stimulation that club and Federation work promised probably was one of its attractions for WFWC leaders.

As educated women, many Federation leaders flirted, at least for a time, with nondomestic goals and expectations. As a group, they married a year or two later than American women generally (twenty-four and twenty-two years old, respectively).[3] And the available information indicates that a substantial portion worked outside the home, at least for a while (see Table 8). Eleven women were working while they served in the Federation: the six unmarried women with careers, and five married women.

Many WFWC leaders held wage-paying jobs before they began their Federation work. Frequently these women held their jobs until they married, and some continued working for a time after marriage. One women was forced by her family's poverty to work as a store clerk when she was a teenager. But teaching drew the largest number; fifteen WFWC leaders worked as educators at some time before they took up Federation activities. Most worked in public schools; one was a college music instructor; another taught at Oberlin College, then joined the faculty of Whitewater Normal School. Two served as assistant principals and two as principals.

TABLE 7

Education

Type	Number of WFWC Leaders
College	17
Normal School	5
Special Art/ Music Study	5
Graduate Work	3
Medical School	1

TABLE 8

Occupations of WFWC Leaders

Employed Prior to WFWC Service		*Employed During WFWC Service*	
Educator	15	Educator	5
Store Clerk	1	Businesswoman	3
		Editor	1
		Physician	1
		Library Organizer	1

Note: The total number of WFWC leaders known to have held paid employment is twenty-five (37.9 percent of the total sample). Two educators prior to WFWC activity were businesswomen during their WFWC service. Women who had essentially the same job before and during their Federation activity are included in the latter list.

More than one-third of the sixty-six women in the leadership sample held jobs at some time. Here again, the information is incomplete, suggesting that this figure could well be significantly higher. And in more than education and employment did WFWC leaders have nondomestic experiences. They participated in a variety of civic activities and organizations, expressing their leadership abilities in these other organizations as well, for example, founding local chapters and holding offices at the local, state, and even national levels. (See Table 9 for a summary of organizational activities.)

Many WFWC leaders were actively involved in some kind of church work. Membership in the women's group or auxiliary of the church was especially common. Others taught in Sunday school; a few played the organ or sang for the church; and some worked for the church missionary society. Church work may have been an important first step into organizational work for these women.[4] The tradition of women's active participation in their churches was established; such work raised the fewest objections in even conservative communities. At the same time, when Federation leaders became involved in clubs and other organizations, they did not abandon church activities. For example, one woman was president, when she died in 1921, of the Women's Guild of her Episcopal church. Another WFWC leader, who had a lengthy Federation career, worked for the Sunday school and women's missionary society of the Presbyterian church in the 1930s.

Membership in patriotic organizations was as common and probably as respectable as church work. Many women were involved in hereditary organizations like the Daughters of the American Revolution and the Colonial Dames. Others were members of patriotic societies like the Woman's Relief Corps and the Auxiliary of the American Legion. The popularity of memberships in hereditary organizations among WFWC leaders is another indication of their ethnic background and perhaps social class. As in all the organizations they joined, WFWC leaders exercised their leadership capabilities in hereditary organizations. Some founded local chapters; at least ten held local offices, five served in state positions, and two held national offices.

As with church work, several women did their first organizational work in patriotic associations. Strathearn's first work was for the Woman's Relief Corps, and Jessie Hooper held her first office in a local DAR chapter. Hooper was reluctant to accept it at first, and did so with the encouragement of her husband, who it seems was generally supportive of her public activities.[5]

World War I provided another opportunity for the expression of patriotic sentiments, and many WFWC leaders participated in civilian war service. Many were drawn to state and county women's committees, which coordinated women's war activities. Others worked with the Red Cross or for governmental agencies, or participated in Liberty Loan drives. WFWC leaders became involved in war work in a variety of capacities. As organized clubwomen, participation in community drives and war projects came naturally. The president of the WFWC sat on the Wisconsin Woman's Committee because of her office; two other Wisconsin Federation leaders were members of the Woman's Committee by virtue of their presidency of statewide women's organizations. And the women with professional expertise in home economics were called on in the effort to conserve food.

Twenty-three WFWC leaders were drawn to the suffrage fight. Five were antisuffragists,[6] and at least three of them were officers in the Wisconsin Association Opposed to Woman Suffrage. Eighteen women joined organizations working for woman suffrage.[7] Fourteen belonged to the Wisconsin Woman Suffrage Association; five worked for the Political Equality League, which was active in the 1912 referendum campaign. Others belonged to local and county suffrage groups. Federation leaders held an impressive range of leadership positions in suffrage groups, too. In 1930, the League of Women Voters (LWV) placed a memorial plaque in its Washington offices commemorating the fifteen Wisconsin women most instrumental in the Wisconsin suffrage fight. Five of these women were also WFWC leaders.[8] And three leaders were involved in the prosuffrage fight nationally, helping in the suffrage campaigns of other states and lobbying in Washington for the federal amendment. Finally, nine WFWC leaders became active in the LWV, the suffrage association's successor following the suffrage victory.

In smaller numbers than their suffrage, patriotic, or church work, WFWC leaders were active in still more societies and associations. For example, ten women were involved in fraternal organizations like the Eastern Star, Greek Letter societies, and the PEO Sisterhood (a secret society auxiliary to no male organization). Others supported organizations for the promotion of special interests. For instance, several Federation leaders belonged to historical associations, some maintaining multiple memberships in the Wisconsin State Historical Society, the Wisconsin Archaeological Society, and county historical societies. Several of the professional women in the leadership sample kept one foot firmly planted in the world of professional organizations. These women did not merely keep their names on the membership lists of such societies, but served in a variety of positions. The first and second women presidents of the Wisconsin Teachers Association were WFWC leaders (Rose Swart and Mary

Bradford). Abby Marlatt held several offices in the American Home Economics Association, as well as membership in the American Chemical Society, the Association for the Advancement of Science, and the Association of Land Grant Colleges and Universities. And some Federation leaders belonged to reform organizations especially attractive to women, such as the WCTU, the Consumers' League, and peace societies.[9]

The roster of organizations that had perhaps only one or two WFWC leaders as members is luxurious in its length and variety. A Milwaukee woman was a board member of the city's Woman's Industrial Exchange; a Waukesha woman belonged to her city's Municipal League. Federation leaders participated in organizations as diverse as the Wisconsin Anti-Tuberculosis Association, the American Association of University Women, the Dane County Humane Society, and the National Conference of Christians and Jews. Several WFWC leaders were active in the Wisconsin Conference of Charities and Corrections (later the Conference of Social Workers), which brought together Wisconsin citizens from many professions and organizations concerned with community welfare. Charlotte Witter was president of this organization for four years. It is probably no accident that the interests embodied in the range of societies to which WFWC leaders belonged is reminiscent of the diverse activities of the Wisconsin Federation itself. Some of the other organizations that WFWC leaders belonged to were the Social Hygiene Association, Federated Charities (of various cities), the Oshkosh Ladies Benevolent Society, the PTA, National Child Labor Committee, and the Friends of Our Native Landscape of Wisconsin.

TABLE 9

Organizational and Civic Activity of WFWC Leaders

Activity	Number of WFWC Leaders
Church Work	19
Patriotic/Hereditary Organizations[a]	19
Hereditary Organizations	16
Patriotic Organizations	4
War Work/Red Cross[a]	18
Woman's Committee	9
Red Cross	7
Other War Projects	8
Suffrage Work	23
Prosuffrage	18
Antisuffrage	5
Fraternal Organizations	10
Historical Societies	6
Professional Societies	4
Woman's Christian Temperance Union	4
Peace Activities	3
Consumers' League	3
Other Organizations	17
Members of Boards, Commissions, etc.	22

[a]Some women participated in activities falling into more than one of the subcategories.

At least a quarter of Wisconsin Federation leaders held official civic appointments or served as members of the bodies responsible for directing various community institutions. For example, they helped direct libraries, public schools and colleges, an orphanage, a museum, and a local YWCA. Some served on citizens' commissions; others were appointed to the Wisconsin Board of Managers of World's Fairs. WFWC leaders' appointments to at least some of these positions reflect the contacts they had made with political figures. For example, Lucy Morris and Theodora Youmans were selected by Governor La Follette to serve on the Wisconsin Board of Managers of the St. Louis World's Fair. Other leaders' political contacts were perhaps at the more local level, and in part may have derived from the visibility and experience they got from club work.

WFWC leaders became known to their communities as civic leaders and, at least in their obituaries, received praise for their public work. For instance, editors of the *Eau Claire Leader* devoted a commemorative editorial to Jennie Shoemaker when she died. They praised her civic contributions highly: "for many years there was not a worthwhile project in the city of Eau Claire that Mrs. Shoemaker was not leading. It was inconceivable to start something without seeking her support and, once it was obtained, the chance of the project's success was immeasurably increased." Mary Connor's obituary noted that she was "famed for her neighborliness and community work."[10] At least some of this community recognition grew from work these women undertook with their clubs. Yet sometimes the club origins of such projects were forgotten, while the civic contributions were remembered. For instance, on hearing of Mary Hobbins's death in Florida in 1935, a major Wisconsin newspaper printed a commemorative editorial, lauding her fund-raising activities for Madison hospitals and her leadership in the Madison Associated Charities. The paper failed to note that these were ventures of the Madison Woman's Club, in which this WFWC leader was active.[11]

Thus, the available information suggests a composite picture of WFWC leaders. As a group, they were financially, socially, and educationally advantaged. Despite their ideological commitment to the domestic sphere, and their real, though comparatively small, family responsibilities, they were active participants in an essentially nondomestic, public realm. Many had been employed, at least for a time. And they found organizational activities and community works an appropriate and attractive way to express their ambitions and ideals. But such a composite picture obscures the differences among WFWC leaders. Many of these women can be distinguished in terms of

A founder and first president of the Wisconsin Federation of Women's Clubs, Lucy Morris, maintained membership in more than one club, as did many of her colleagues. Her interest in literature led to her appointment to the Wisconsin Library Commission and her determination to make books available to the public. (State Historical Society of Wisconsin.)

differing types or patterns of leadership. They accepted their prominent roles in Wisconsin Federation for divergent and definable reasons. Such different rationales for WFWC participation signify various types of contributions WFWC leaders made to their organizations.

Federation leadership attracted some women as a natural extension of their serious, almost overriding commitment to the club movement. These women usually maintained memberships in more than one local club. And their nonclub activities either resembled or grew out of the same impulse as their club work. Lucy Morris, a founder and first president of the WFWC, was such a woman. Wisconsin clubwomen called Morris the "little mother of the Federation," in honor of her long devotion to the WFWC, which lasted well past 1920.[12] Morris organized the Athena Club of Berlin, Wisconsin, and served as its president for more than twenty-five years. She belonged to another Berlin study club, the Friends-in-Council.

Club work partly satisfied Morris's special interest in literature. She became an expert on Shakespeare and prepared study pamphlets on this and other topics for club use. Her early leadership of Wisconsin clubwomen led to her appointment to the Wisconsin Library Commission in 1896.[13] In her twenty years' service on the commission, Morris worked to increase the availability of books to the public. Club and WFWC work also tapped Morris's extensive gifts as an organizer of women and her carefully stated but real concern for the rights of women. Morris expressed this concern graciously, humorously, but nonetheless forcefully in her presidential address at the 1889 convention. This convention met in a church, and the clubwomen were welcomed by Reverend Mueller. Morris thanked Reverend Mueller for his kind greeting, noting the necessary brevity of his words. She continued:

> It is possible that Paul, in promulgating his celebrated phrase "let your women keep silent in the churches," foresaw with prophetic vision exactly such an occasion as the present, when the tyranny of women would limit a man—the rightful occupant of a pulpit—to a five minute talk, and appropriate for themselves, individually, anywhere from ten to thirty minutes. But, if the great apostle hoped to forestall such untoward circumstances, his dreams were vain, for here we are in control, and many of us refuse to say, "I come not here to talk." Allow me to remind you, however, that, whatever may be asserted regarding the *tongueiness* of women, they are still as they have ever been "the listeners of the world," as an inspection of any church or lecture-room audience proves; also, that there is in the dictionary such a word as tongue-man defined as a talkative person, but no tongue-woman.[14]

These same talents and concerns underlay Morris's work for woman suffrage and, later, her activity organizing LWV chapters. She also coordinated the civilian war service of Green Lake County's women and was a long-time supporter of the peace movement, having joined the Women's International Peace Association in 1877. But her first love was the club movement.[15]

Morris's successor to the presidency, Ella Neville, also found club work and WFWC leadership an apt expression of her primary interests. A charter member of the Green Bay Shakespeare Club in 1877, Neville later helped found the Green Bay Woman's Club, a department club, and was a leader in it until her death in 1935. Active in the Wisconsin Federation well beyond the second decade of the twentieth century, Neville also served on the General Federation's home economics committee. In 1888, after helping to establish the public library in Green Bay, Neville began five decades of service on the library board. An early promoter of WFWC activity in landmarks and history, Neville supported the Wisconsin State Historical Society and the Brown County Historical Society. She was the impetus behind the City Beautiful Committee of the Green Bay Woman's Club, and this interest in civic beautification led to her membership on the State Committee of One Hundred for the Protection of Roadside Beauty, and participation in the American Civic Association.[16]

Clara Humphrey never held the WFWC presidency, but she was a district vice president and then served as WFWC treasurer from 1908 to 1910. Afterward, she received several committee appointments, including one to the club extension committee, an appropriate place for a woman devoted to the club movement and club organizations. A charter member (1889) of the Whitewater Emerson Club, she later presided over the Whitewater city federation of clubs, which organized the women's clubs of Whitewater for collaboration on community projects. Humphrey remained active in the city federation, and for eighteen years directed its health committee, overseeing the sale of antituberculosis stamps and helping bring the first chest clinics to Whitewater. Humphrey also found a comfortable club movement niche in the First District Federation of Women's Clubs, a district auxiliary of the WFWC. She helped organize it in 1902 and served on its board until 1934. Humphrey's other major community work spanned more than twenty years as secretary of the Whitewater chapter of the Red Cross. Red Cross interests dovetailed nicely with her work on the health committee of the city federation of clubs.[17]

Federation leaders like Morris, Neville, and Humphrey channeled their many interests through club work and committed much of their talents to the club movement. Although they participated in other organizations, the club movement held a primary place in their lives. Other women integrated club work, and its extension, WFWC leadership, with other activities, to express and secure their prominent place in their communities as members of families of eminent reputations. These women tended to participate in respectable, noncontroversial activities, usually church work and patriotic societies. Emma Crosby, Della Emerson, and Carrie Edwards exemplify this type of leadership.

Emma Crosby, Federation president from 1910 to 1912, was highly respected in her long-time home of Racine. Her obituary noted that she came from a prominent, old family of Racine, and she and her husband, a railroad executive and businessman, were praised for their contributions to the city's development. A wealthy woman, Crosby gave generously to the Wisconsin and General Federations, including the Loan Fund for Higher Education, the GFWC's Endowment Fund, and a WFWC collection for flood victims in Black River Falls in 1912. The writers of Crosby's obituary suggested that her social prominence and material advantages were not wasted: "Mrs. Crosby's way of life found expression in numerous affiliations of responsibility." They cited her leadership in the DAR, work in the First Presbyterian Church of Racine, and activity in the Red Cross, as well as her club work to prove their point.[18] A founder and leader of the Racine Woman's Club, Crosby served for a short while on the Wisconsin Woman Suffrage Association's advisory board. Aside from this suffrage activity, Crosby's organizational involvements were socially orthodox.[19]

Like Crosby, Della Emerson, WFWC vice president and later vice president of the first district, came from an old, respected family. Her father was a city founder of Beloit. Her husband, also from a pioneer family, was the community's leading druggist. While Mr. Emerson served as a trustee of Beloit College, the Congregational Church, and the YMCA, Della Emerson became "a leader in the social and club life" of Beloit. Charter member of the Coterie Club and member of the Saturday Club, Emerson helped organize the Beloit Federation of Women's Clubs and twice was elected its president. She rounded off her community participation with memberships in the Beloit DAR and the women's organization of the Congregational Church.[20] Emerson's organizational work lived up to community expectations regarding the respectability of a city founder's daughter and leading businessman's wife.

Antisuffragist Carrie Edwards, seventh president of the WFWC, was one of the Federation's more politically conservative leaders. Her conservatism stands out among the conservative style of clubwomen generally and is apparent in her presidential addresses at the 1909 and 1910 conventions. In 1910, she defined the goals of clubwomen: "We want a harvest of honest citizenship, of manly boys, and modest girls, happy workingmen and women, sanitary homes, clean morals and religious influences."[21] Edwards's club work included charter membership and three presidencies of the Oshkosh Twentieth Century Club, leadership in the Oshkosh Women's Reading Club, and WFWC service from 1902 to 1916. She combined her extensive club work with membership in the local DAR and the Ladies' Society of an Oshkosh Congregational Church. She expanded her public service by serving on the Oshkosh library and school boards, and by participating in the Oshkosh Ladies Benevolent Society, which maintained a home for elderly women.[22] Her husband, Richard Edwards, was a highly successful Oshkosh businessman, who began with a retail grocery business and ended with lumber and timber interests in four states.

Hence, Edwards, Crosby, and Emerson's participation in the club movement contributed to a set of activities that maintained their reputations as responsible, respectable, and prominent women of the community. Committed to the survival and stability of the WFWC, they worked hard for it. And they were not the only Wisconsin Federation leaders whose Federation activities advanced goals not deriving directly from the club movement itself. Many WFWC leaders were drawn to the Wisconsin Federation (and perhaps the club movement) as a way to further concerns that they had given other institutional and organizational expression. Although these women devoted considerable time and energy to the clubs and the Federation, these were in some sense secondary to their other activities. They typically held standing committee memberships that reflected these other interests.

For example, the professional women among WFWC leaders used their Wisconsin Federation activities to further their professional goals. Ellen Sabin was one of Wisconsin's foremost women educators. She began her career teaching school, first in Wisconsin, and then in Oregon. After three years as superintendent of Portland's schools, Sabin returned to Wisconsin in 1890, to serve as president of Downer College, a women's school. Five years later, she guided its merger with Milwaukee Institute, and from then until her retirement in 1921, she was president of Milwaukee-Downer College. Sabin's professional activities also included membership in the National Education Association, and from 1919 to 1923, service on the Wisconsin Board of Education.[23]

Sabin, a suffragist, was active in women's organizations as well, including two influential Milwaukee department clubs, the Milwaukee College Endowment Association, and the Woman's Club of Wisconsin. During much of her tenure as Milwaukee-Downer's president, Sabin served on WFWC committees that matched her professional expertise and aims: the education, home economics, and loan fund for higher education committees. Sabin believed that women were best suited to employment in certain "feminine" occupations, especially homemaking, teaching, and nursing. She developed her college along these lines, nurturing its programs in education, home economics, and nursing. This approach to women's education was well understood and supported by Wisconsin clubwomen, who gave material as well as moral backing to Sabin's goals, such as the domestic science chair endowed by the WFWC. Sabin's participation in the Wisconsin Federation followed closely her professional objectives: improved but gender-specific education for women and acceptance of home economics as an academic field.[24]

Mary Bradford was another professional educator among the WFWC leadership. When the death of her husband in 1881 left her a widow with a young child, Bradford resumed a career teaching in public schools. In 1894, she began teaching in normal schools and remained there until 1910, when she went to Kenosha to serve for twelve years as superintendent of public schools. Like Sabin, Bradford's professional life included memberships in professional organizations. In 1911, Bradford became the second woman elected to the presidency of the Wisconsin Teachers Association; and almost a decade later she accepted a similar post in the National Council of Administrative Women in Education.

Bradford made a special place for herself in Wisconsin educational history as a promoter of innovations, many of which we now take for granted. As the superintendent in Kenosha, Bradford introduced kindergartens, home economics, and industrial arts throughout the school system; opened a summer school; and made special facilities available to children with physical and learning handicaps.[25] Her innovative thinking brought her some public criticism, and part of her task was to build support for educational reform.[26] A member of several women's clubs, Bradford used her eight years on the Wisconsin Federation's education committee to help gain public support for her ideas. The reports she wrote for this committee, for instance, were designed to tap into clubwomen's receptivity to school innovations.[27]

President of Milwaukee-Downer College, Ellen Sabin, typified Wisconsin Federation of Women's Clubs career women by serving on committees that furthered her professional experience and goals. Throughout her life she worked for the acceptance of home economics as an academic field and for the improvement of women's education in appropriate "feminine" fields. (State Historical Society of Wisconsin.)

79

The WFWC had a special niche for professional women working in the new field of home economics. After receiving a Master's degree in chemistry in 1890, Abby Marlatt organized domestic science programs at Utah State Agricultural College and then at the Manual Training School in Providence, Rhode Island. In 1909, Marlatt left Providence for a position in the home economics department at the University of Wisconsin in Madison. She became the program's director in 1913, and when she retired twenty years later, she left the university with one of the strongest home economics programs in the country.[28]

Her success came with some assistance from clubwomen. Shortly after Marlatt came to Wisconsin, she commenced almost a decade of service on the Federation's home economics committee. In 1916, the committee's chair gave Marlatt special credit for shaping the policy and carrying out the work of her committee. Through this committee, clubwomen materially supported the growth and acceptability of home economics as an academic field, important to Marlatt as one of the discipline's pioneers. And clubwomen gave Marlatt a big hand in getting the legislative appropriations with which she built her home economics program.[29]

Clubwomen's commitment to establishing libraries attracted the attention of librarian Lutie Stearns. After teaching school briefly, in 1888 Stearns accepted a job as a librarian at the Milwaukee Public Library. In 1894, she helped draft the legislation creating the Wisconsin Free Library Commission, which facilitated the organization of free public libraries throughout the state. For two years Sterns served as an unpaid member of the Commission, and then in 1897, she became its first paid staff member. She worked with the Commission until 1914, traveling to cities and towns across the state, speaking to citizens, and helping them establish local public libraries. Stearns also directed the Commission's department of traveling libraries, inaugurated in 1903.[30]

Stearns belonged to several Milwaukee women's clubs. She attended the founding convention of the WFWC, and served for thirteen years on the Federation's library committee, and for two years as district vice president. Stearns used her WFWC work to aid her library organizing efforts. Sensing the potential contributions of the WFWC in the promotion of libraries, she arranged to have Lucy Morris appointed to the Free Library Commission.[31] Well respected by WFWC members, Stearns frequently lectured to women's clubs and addressed district conventions on the subject of libraries. One brief

A librarian at the Milwaukee Public Library, Lutie Stearns helped draft the legislation which created the Wisconsin Free Library Commission. As its first staff member, she traveled around Wisconsin giving lectures and helping establish local libraries. (State Historical Society of Wisconsin.)

history of Stearns's library work notes that "she had a staff of one: Lutie Stearns." Actually, she had a staff of hundreds: Wisconsin clubwomen.[32]

Several WFWC leaders worked mainly as volunteers rather than paid professionals, such as Julia Lapham and Mattie Van Ostrand, members of the Federation's landmarks committee. Lapham was the daughter of Increase Lapham, a Wisconsin pioneer, scientist, and founder of the weather bureau. Lapham cared for her father's extensive papers on his studies of natural history, geology and meteorology, and worked on a history of his life. She herself became an "unofficial" expert on the history of Wisconsin and her home county, and wrote some historical papers, which she sometimes read to women's clubs. She collected historically interesting materials and saw to their proper disposition to museums, archives, and historical societies. She was a founding member and secretary of the Waukesha County Historical Society and a member of the Wisconsin Archaeological Society. An active member of her local club, she served on the Federation's landmarks committee for nine years and chaired it for almost half of these.[33]

In Lapham's final two years on the landmarks committee, she served with Mattie Van Ostrand. Van Ostrand's memberships in a wide variety of hereditary associations permitted her to do extensive genealogical and historical work. She also held offices in the Wisconsin Archaeological Society and Wisconsin Historical Society. Her own research on local and national history made its way into club publications and lectures. Van Ostrand belonged to the Madison Women's Club, at one time heading its history department. She chaired the Wisconsin Federation's history and landmarks committee for four of the eight years she served on it. For both Lapham and Van Ostrand, Federation leadership was one of several means for carrying on their work in history.[34]

Several other WFWC leaders used their leadership roles to promote particular social and political changes. These women were devoted members of reform societies. Vie Campbell, for example, was no stranger to women's organizations. An early supporter of suffrage, Campbell was vice president of the Wisconsin Suffrage Association in the mid-1880s. Even more active in the WCTU, Campbell held a variety of state offices, including the presidency from 1892 to 1898. In the twentieth century, she was a WCTU state and national organizer and lecturer. But it was Campbell's interests in the Consumers' League that brought her to WFWC leadership. In 1894, she was the superintendent of the Wisconsin WCTU's department on the "relation of temperance to capital and labor," and her 1895 presidential address included a discussion of workers' problems. Campbell later pursued such concerns in the Wisconsin Consumers' League. Her WFWC service consisted almost entirely of eight years' membership on the Federation's Consumers' League Committee.[35]

Edna Chynoweth, too, spent a lifetime in women's reform organizations. Chynoweth attended the University of Wisconsin when it first opened its doors to women. She joined the WCTU and served as the Wisconsin treasurer in the late 1880s. A highly respected woman suffrage proponent, she was the president of the Dane County Equal Suffrage League and a member of the Wisconsin Woman Suffrage Association, serving for a time as its correspondence secretary. A supporter of the women's peace movement, Chynoweth founded the Madison branch of the Women's International League for Peace and Freedom.[36]

Chynoweth, a devotee of Progressivism, was also an early WFWC leader. A founding member and president (1901-1903) of the influential Madison Woman's Club, Chynoweth helped Lucy Morris, in 1895, organize the Wisconsin Federation. She served on its standing education and policy committees and was elected a vice president in 1902. The WFWC was yet another women's organization where Chynoweth promoted her political goals. For example, in 1900, when the WFWC took one of its first steps toward suffrage support by creating a special committee to obtain the legislation to make women's school suffrage a reality, Chynoweth was appointed to the committee. A few years later, she used her opening address to the convention to introduce delegates to the peace issue.[37]

Lutie Stearns also was committed to the Progressive point of view. She credited Jane Addams as being a special inspiration to her and, as an older woman, remarked: "I've been called a 'radical' and 'a communist,' but I recall that Susan B. Anthony was termed 'an old hen' and Jane Addams was designated by an Illinois Commander of the National Guard as 'the most dangerous person in America,' so I'm in good company."[38] In 1914, Stearns resigned from the Free Library Commission to pursue a career as a lecturer and writer. Her speeches promoted her social and political ideas, including woman suffrage, the peace movement, workers' rights, and temperance. Stearns frequently lectured to women's clubs, having established a reputation among clubwomen as a WFWC leader.[39]

No WFWC leader combined her Federation responsibilities with active support for reform better than Sophie Gudden. Gudden's chief concerns lay in the Consumers' League and prosuffrage fights. Her Consumers' League work dated from the turn of the century and included the presidency and later the vice presidency of the Wisconsin Consumers' League, and a vice presidency in the National Consumers' League. Her suffrage work began around the 1912 referendum campaign, with the Wisconsin Political Equality League (PEL). After the referendum lost, the PEL merged with the Wisconsin Woman Suffrage Association (WWSA) under the latter name, and Gudden worked for the WWSA. For both the PEL and WWSA, Gudden traveled about the state speaking about suffrage and did press work, supplying the Wisconsin papers with suffrage information and articles. A native of Germany, Gudden sought especially to bring the prosuffrage cause to Wisconsin's German community. Her Consumers' League work convinced Gudden that woman suffrage was essential to bettering the conditions of the working class.

A resident of Oshkosh, Gudden was a member of its Leisure Hour Art and Twentieth Century clubs. Her Federation work included four years (1900-1904) as head of the art interchange committee and then six years as chair of the Consumers' League committee (1904-1910). A skilled organizer, Gudden used her WFWC work to promote first the Consumers' League and then woman suffrage. She spoke about these at club meetings throughout the state and at district and WFWC conventions, and she introduced relevant resolutions at conventions. Although her tenure in WFWC posts was drawing to a close as she became actively involved in the suffrage battle, her Federation reputation continued to give her entree to agitate for suffrage among clubwomen.[40]

Gudden's personal energy supported an extensive and tiring schedule of speaking tours, legislative lobbying, press work, and grassroots organizing. Her accomplishments stand forth especially in light of several physical handicaps (mobility and visual problems) and some sort of serious physical illness that she endured through her suffrage campaigning. Gudden's quiet heroism is revealed in a letter to suffrage leader Ada James during the 1912 campaign. "Sometimes I get simply heartsick," Gudden wrote, describing some recent discouragements, and concluded, "Today my courage is at twenty-eight below zero, but [it] never stays long at this temperature."[41]

Professional women like Sabin and Marlatt, reformers like Chynoweth and Gudden, and those seriously committed to avocations like Van Ostrand and Lapham found WFWC leadership one of several means to advance their particular nonclub objectives. The WFWC was enriched by the special expertise provided by such women, who also helped maintain vital links between the WFWC and other organizations and institutions. The WFWC gained similar benefits from leaders who incorporated WFWC and club activities in extensive public careers. Several Federation leaders carved out careers in social service. Mary Connor founded the Token Creek Library Association, a study club that provided library services to the town of Token Creek. Connor later joined the Madison Woman's Club. She also organized Catholic women, first by founding the Catholic Woman's Club of Madison and serving as its first president from 1914 to 1916. In 1916, she organized the State Council of Catholic Women, again accepting the presidency. Her WFWC work included four years as district vice president, two years on the health committee, and five years on the club extension committee.

Connor listed her occupation as "social worker" in a 1921 Wisconsin Alumni directory. She used her club activities and contacts as a basis for this social service career and became known for civic work in Dane County. With the cooperation of Catholic and Protestant churches, Connor conducted a survey assessing the spiritual needs of the people in state institutions. She also directed a survey of the conditions among Native Americans on Wisconsin reservations, and at the time of her death was active in a movement to aid Wisconsin Native Americans.[42]

Frances Chandler's obituary remembered her as an "active welfare and charity worker." Chandler was a charter member and several times president of the Racine Woman's Club. Her WFWC service included the vice presidency from 1916 to 1920, followed by a two-year term as president. She also was elected president of the Ladies Auxiliary of her Presbyterian church several times. With other Racine residents Chandler successfully lobbied for the introduction of kindergartens and music instruction in the city's schools. For thirty years she served on the Board of Directors of an orphanage and presided over this board from 1927 until her death in 1933. Distressed by the plight of young women without homes, she also was president of the Board of Directors of the YWCA. And from 1914 to 1930, Chandler led the local Red Cross. With good reason, her obituary mourned her death as one of Racine's "most active workers in the church, club life and local charities," who gave "much of her time during a long period of her life in the interest of the unfortunate."[43]

Sophie Strathearn's substantial contributions to club and Wisconsin Federation work were part of her impressive career in a variety of public service activities. Strathearn was a charter member of the Kaukauna Woman's Club in 1897, and somewhat later was its president for eleven years.[44] Her WFWC positions included recording secretary, district vice president,

Federation vice president and the presidency from 1912 to 1914, as well as membership on a variety of committees. She also was active in the GFWC.

But club work was only part of Strathearn's public life. Her public career began in the 1880s as an organizer for the Wisconsin Woman's Relief Corps. She later held a variety of positions in the Wisconsin WRC, including the presidency from 1910 to 1911; in the latter year she accepted a position in the National Woman's Relief Corps. Strathearn also was active in the Consumers' League, serving as Wisconsin president from 1908 to 1911; she was thus well prepared for her Federation work.[45] In 1911, Strathearn was considered for an appointment to the State Board of Control of Charitable, Penal and Reform Institutions, which she wanted badly but did not receive.

Strathearn's activity continued well past her fifty-fifth birthday in 1920, when she accepted the presidency of the North Side Relief and Family Welfare Society in Manitowoc, a position she held for more than fifteen years. A vice presidency of the National Consumers' League came her way in 1921. In 1920, Strathearn began sixteen years of work as superintendent of Sunday schools in her Presbyterian church, and she was president of the Woman's Synodical Missionary Society from 1931 to 1937. During the Depression, she served on the governor's citizens' unemployment commission.[46]

Strathearn, Connor, and Chandler created lengthy social service careers by filling a variety of positions open to women. Other WFWC leaders constructed public careers that in varying degrees became increasingly political.

Theodora Youmans was one of the outstanding leaders of the Wisconsin women's movement. A member and three times president of the Waukesha Woman's Club, she held several WFWC positions, including the presidency from 1900 to 1902. Thereafter, she served on a variety of committees, among them the civil service reform and citizenship committee (the latter established after women won the vote), which reflected her political interests.

Youmans, who had a lengthy career as an assistant editor of a Waukesha paper, used her club contacts to advance the cause of suffrage. Youmans did press work for both the Political Equality League and the WWSA. When the two merged in 1913, Youmans agreed to accept the presidency, which she held until suffrage was won. She also edited the *Wisconsin Citizen*, the publication of the WWSA, and in 1915 went to Buffalo for a time to help in the New York suffrage campaign. During World War I, her presidency of the WWSA brought her membership on the Woman's Committee, and she did extensive civilian war work. After the suffrage battle was won, Youmans became an officer in the League of Women Voters.[47]

An influential member of the Wisconsin Federation of Women's Clubs and its president from 1902-1904, Theodora Youmans, also had a career as an assistant editor of a Waukesha newspaper. An avid suffragist, she used her editorial experience and club contacts to promote women's right to vote. (State Historical Society of Wisconsin.)

87

Youmans had friends in politics when woman suffrage was something of a laughing matter. In 1905, Governor La Follette appointed her to the Board of Normal School Regents, a position she held for ten years. During this time, she also served as one of the five members of Wisconsin's Board of Managers for the St. Louis Fair and helped found the Wisconsin Anti-Tuberculosis Association and the Waukesha County Historical Society.[48]

With the suffrage victory won, Youmans turned to Republican party politics. She was a member of the Republican National Committee in 1920 and later became involved in an organization of Republican women, serving as its vice president in 1929. And in 1924, she sought a seat in the state senate, but lost in the primary.[49]

Like Youmans, fellow suffragist and Federation leader Jessie Jack Hooper became active in party politics, but as a Democrat. Hooper's public career began in the 1890s, in her home of Oshkosh. Hooper belonged to the Twentieth Century Club, the Woman's Parliamentary Law Club, and the Business Woman's Club. Agitating for the first kindergarten in Oshkosh was Hooper's earliest community project, and she later helped initiate Oshkosh's visiting nurse program and raised funds for a tuberculosis sanitarium in Winnebago County. Hooper recalled that the first office she ever held was regent of a local DAR. Several years later, in 1913, she was elected president of the Twentieth Century Club, and she served as an officer in the Oshkosh Ladies Benevolent Society. For twenty years, Hooper was a member of the Oshkosh Planning Commission.[50]

After 1910, Hooper's public career took her farther afield. Hooper joined the WWSA shortly after 1900 and then worked with the PEL in the 1912 referendum campaign, after lobbying in 1910 for the legislation calling for the referendum. She then became active in the "merged" WWSA, doing her most important work as chair of its legislative committee. Her skills attracted the attention of national suffrage leaders, and Hooper served on the board of NAWSA. With Carrie Chapman Catt and Anna Howard Shaw, Hooper campaigned in Washington, D.C., for the federal suffrage amendment.[51]

It was during her active suffrage years that Hooper held WFWC offices: recording secretary from 1912 to 1914 and legislative committee member from 1916 to 1918. During World War I, she did civilian war work for the Red Cross, in food conservation and Liberty Loan Drives, and as an organizer for the Wisconsin Woman's Committee. At this time, she also was involved in the Wisconsin Conference of Charities and Corrections and served on its social legislation committee from 1919 to 1920.[52]

Jessie Jack Hooper was active in many clubs and later in party politics. Her public career began in the 1890's by agitating for Oshkosh's first kindergarten. In 1922 she ran against Robert LaFollette for the U.S. Senate. (State Historical Society of Wisconsin.)

Throughout this period of her life, Hooper was especially drawn to legislative work, and she developed considerable skill as a lobbyist. After 1920, politics occupied the bulk of her time. She was the first president of the Wisconsin League of Women Voters, and during her 1920 to 1922 term of office, the LWV worked for legislation to aid women and children, including laws to raise the age of consent, permit women to sit on juries, give women equal guardianship over their children, and increase the size of mothers' pensions to poor women.[53]

Hooper resigned her LWV presidency to work for the peace movement and the Democratic Party. In 1924, she helped Carrie Catt organize the Conference on the Cause and the Cure of War. In 1928, she submitted to this organization a comprehensive plan for peace, which was voted the most practical of all plans submitted. Secretary of the Conference from 1928 to 1932, in the latter year Hooper headed a women's delegation that presented women's peace petitions to the Geneva Peace Conference.

In the meantime, Hooper maintained a somewhat unsuccessful political career. In 1922, the Democratic Party drafted her to run against La Follette for the United States Senate on a platform favoring prohibition; a constitutional amendment against child labor; and international cooperation to maintain world peace. Hooper lost to the popular La Follette. In 1934, she ran for the Wisconsin Senate, losing in the primary. A year later, Hooper died of cancer.[54]

The leaders of the Wisconsin Federation met a range of public and private responsibilities. Some had so many that finding time for them all was a task in itself. Sophie Gudden frequently mentioned the problem posed by her domestic responsibilities, telling Ada James, for instance, that she would "die if I do not get a permanent maid soon."[55] Theodora Youmans poignantly explained her situation to James in her initial refusal to accept the presidency of the WWSA:

> You don't know how much I want to do what you want me to do. It's such a chance to help in a big thing, a thing that will affect all women who came after, making their lives I believe a little easier, a little better. And it's the kind of work I like to do. But I can't do it—there isn't any use pretending for a moment that I can. My life is already over-crowded, my strength appropriated to its last bit. With my newspaper work, my housekeeping, my normal school work, my club work, and an astonishing number of incidentals—I have reached the limit.[56]

Later, Youmans reconsidered. WFWC leaders seemed unable to resist the pull of the public sphere.

But they faced a society that often felt the need to reassure itself that these were true women, no matter what their public contributions. When Mary Sawyer, president of the WFWC from 1904 to 1906, died in 1910, her obituary noted her fine intellectual ability and organizational skills. Then it continued: "Notwithstanding these interests her domestic affairs were never neglected for her home was her sanctuary. Here it was that the beauty and sweetness of devoted wifehood and motherhood were exhaled [sic]. Here it was that her family and friends were enabled to penetrate the depths of her royal womanhood."[57] As late as 1926, another Wisconsin Federation leader, Mary Rote, received similar treatment, albeit in less florid language. Her obituary described her nondomestic work only after assuring the reader that first in "her heart" came "her home and the little family of her son."[58]

Wisconsin Federation leaders built and presided over an organization ideologically committed to homemaking as woman's truest role. Yet these socially advantaged women were anything but "just wives and mothers." Their experiences went well beyond the domestic world into the realms of education, paid employment, organizational activity, and public responsibilities.

Summary

In 1912, the Wisconsin Federation took part in the dedication ceremonies at the site of the Wisconsin territorial legislature, which the WFWC had purchased to set aside as a landmark. Emma Crosby, Federation president, gave an address that defined her view of the history of women, a view in which she and her fellow clubwomen had a definite place. With the suffrage referendum a few weeks away, Crosby spoke of the intelligent Wisconsin pioneer woman, dreaming of the day when women would participate in the fullest citizenship:

> for the potentialities of a united womanhood were, as yet, hidden vastly deep in the heart of things. It was a voice calling, calling, bidding women come forth and *be* something; to endeavor to discover her own power and her own personality, and to do bravely and unafraid her part in the great social plan. She was to be not a *new* woman, but an *improved* woman, who should help to carry things a step further along the great highway of life.[1]

Faced with a rapidly changing society, clubwomen built on, and reinterpreted, the legacy of their personal history as American women, not redrawing, but broadening the outlines of their present.

Clubwomen of Wisconsin shared much with clubwomen throughout the United States. They shared a justification for their activities and a self-image based on traditional conceptions of feminine temperament and ability. Blair's "domestic feminism" was adopted, both by clubwomen and their nonclub activist contemporaries, because whatever its difficulties, it was readily adapted to the needs of many women and the requirements of many situations. For instance, women of the WCTU justified their fight against liquor as an expression of their duty to protect the home. Settlement workers like Jane Addams believed that the intuitive moral sensitivity of women put them in the forefront of solving human problems. Women's urban reform efforts occurred under the aegis of "municipal housekeeping," the homemaker's natural ability to manage the larger home of the city. The club movement everywhere was composed mostly of multipurpose organizations, whose members came together not with a specific goal, but to learn, and then to do, among those with whom they shared a sense of a common womanhood. Women's clubs everywhere also had an expansive tendency: Study of Shakespeare led to study of municipal problems; study led to activity; small projects led to more complex ventures.

Wisconsin clubwomen were builders and modifiers of community institutions and services. Especially fond of founding and maintaining libraries, WFWC women were grassroots organizers in library promotion efforts. Clubwomen fostered changes in the curriculum and facilities of schools, calling for kindergartens and playgrounds, for instance. In a world that clubwomen felt was becoming too rampantly commercial, WFWC members helped preserve natural and historic landmarks. Their work in public health helped restructure public awareness and social customs in regard to health problems. The work of any one woman's club, in Wisconsin or elsewhere, may seem small or historically insignificant, but the combined efforts of clubwomen gave them an important place in Progressive efforts to transform and modernize urban environments.

Wisconsin clubwomen faced constraints due to their limited financial resources and their disfranchisement, which signaled to male politicians their lack of direct political clout. Through what Beard called "conscious national womanhood," and what Freedman called "women's separate public sphere," activist women everywhere might at least partially overcome such constraints, increasing women's access to power and contributing to changes in the public arena that women thought desirable. But how did women activists, in concrete terms, attempt to implement women's public sphere?

Wisconsin clubwomen built an internally elaborate structure, which provided many leadership positions for women in a world that limited their opportunities within traditional power structures. Talented and ambitious women found positions of power and responsibility not only in their own clubs, but in city and district federations and in the committees and officerships of the state federation. Some even found a place in the General Federation of Women's Clubs. Clubwomen's ritualized friendships helped hold together this sometimes unwieldy organizational machinery. The complex network in which the WFWC enmeshed member clubs compensated for the Federation's inability to compel its members to take a particular action.

Clubwomen also laid the groundwork for opportunities for women outside the club movement's structures, for example, by securing the appointment of women to public positions. Also, club experience frequently gave clubwomen themselves entree to official public roles. Finally, the Wisconsin Federation's relationships with other volunteer organizations were vitally important to its success in creating a public sphere for its members.

The study of Wisconsin Federation leaders, as well as the material on their organization, supports this conception of the construction of the women's public sphere. Federation leaders' education, work experiences, and small families made strict adherence to an ideology that confined them to private, domestic realms difficult, and their class status gave them extra resources with which to create an acceptable escape. Most, if not all WFWC leaders were leaders in their local clubs as well, suggesting their special skills as leaders of women. At least half were members of department clubs or city federations, whose larger-scale, more comprehensive, multiple civic projects offered a greater outlet for their ambitions than did the small-scale ventures associated with self-improvement clubs. With a secure place as leaders in the club movement, many of these women served in and led other volunteer organizations, or even filled official positions. Thus, in operation, women's separate public sphere was not a distinct entity existing side by side in the male public sphere. Rather, it was a set of relationships between male and female public activity, and among female activists, which ensured that women's public activity was not isolated in, or swallowed by, the male-defined public realm.

Wisconsin clubwomen confirm Beard's proposition regarding the efficacy of women's reform work in urban areas, in spite of their disfranchisement. The WFWC also suggests the working value of Freedman's conception of a separate public sphere, and this study gives concrete meaning to the abstract formulation. Were clubwomen feminists, as Blair argues? This question tends to put the historian in the awkward and untenable position of measuring the women of the past by the standards of modern women's ideas, of criticizing the women activists of the turn of the century for not believing in what feminists of today hold to be the key to emancipation. Ideas are important; they can set limits to people's actions. But action redefines ideas, and individuals frequently violate their ideas through their behavior, without realizing the connection. Women's public sphere embodied American women's ideas about their womanhood, as they simultaneously used, contradicted, and modified these ideas, in their search to create a better social order and define their places in it.

Appendix

The following is an alphabetical list of the sixty-six women in the leadership sample. Name, residence, and highest WFWC post ever held are given for each woman. In each case, the source for data on WFWC positions was the convention proceedings, so this is not listed. All census materials are manuscript schedules of the population.

Aylward, Jennie Huenkemeier (Mrs. John A.) Madison, vice president, 1914-1916. Sources: *Wisconsin Alumni Magazine*, vol. 1, December 1899, p. 132. *Madison Democrat*, November 14, 1916, *Wisconsin Necrology*, vol. 16, pp. 2-4. Ellis Baker Usher, *Wisconsin: Its Story and Biography, 1848-1913* (Chicago: Lewis Publishing Company, 1914), vol. 8, p. 2362. McCaul, "Wisconsin Women's War Work," Wisconsin State Census, 1905.

Bardon, Jennie Grant (Mrs. Thomas) Ashland, correspondence secretary, 1989-1900. Sources: *Ashland Press*, November 22, 1939, *Wisconsin Necrology*, vol. 42, pp. 18-19. *Ashland Press*, February 2, 1923, *Wisconsin Necrology*, vol. 21, pp. 4-7. United States Census, 1900.

Barrett, Julia Dennet (Mrs. Edward J.) Sheboygan, recording secretary, 1916-1918. Sources: *Fond du Lac Commonwealth Reporter*, February 28, 1933, *Wisconsin Necrology*, vol. 32, p. 115. Wisconsin State Census, 1915.

Bradford, Mary Davison (Mrs. William R.) Stevens Point; Menomonie; Whitewater; Kenosha, Education Committee, chair, 1904-1906, 1908-1910, 1914-1916. Sources: *Kenosha News*, February 4, 1943, *Wisconsin Necrology*, vol. 48, pp. 188-89. Kohler, *Story of Wisconsin Women*, p. 118. "Information About Mary Davison Bradford," pp. 1-10, Wisconsin State Historical Society, Madison. Dr. G. B. Willis to Crystal Eastman Benedict, letter, September 28, 1912, Ada James Papers, Box 15, Wisconsin State Historical Society, Madison. Wisconsin State Census, 1905.

Brooks, Mabel Smith (Mrs. W. D.) Green Lake, vice president, 1916-1918. Sources: United States Census, 1900. Wisconsin State Census, 1905.

Brown, Alice Louisa (Mrs. Thomas H.) Milwaukee, president, 1902-1904. Sources: *Milwaukee Sentinel*, June 19, 1908, *Wisconsin Necrology*, vol. 10, pp. 63-64. Gregory, *Southeastern Wisconsin*, vol. 3, p. 27. Kohler, *Story of Wisconsin Women*, p. 95. "In Memory of Mrs. Thomas H. Brown," *Proceedings*, 1914, pp. 74-76. United States Census, 1900.

Buell, Martha (Mrs. Charles), president 1906-1908. Sources: *Capital Times*, October 9, 1942, *Wisconsin Necrology*, vol. 47, p. 231. *Capital Times*, February 7, 1942, *Wisconsin Necrology*, vol. 39, p. 189. *Wisconsin Clubwoman*, vol. 23, January/February 1940, pp. 10-11. United States Census, 1900. Wisconsin State Census, 1905.

Campbell, Vie (Mrs. Henry) Evansville, Consumers' League Committee member, 1902-1910. Sources: *Proceedings*, 1905, p. 69. WCTU of Wisconsin, *Annual Reports*, 1892-1907. Graves, "Wisconsin Woman Suffrage Movement," p. 371. Vie Campbell to Theodora Youmans, undated letter, Wisconsin Woman Suffrage Association Papers, Box 11, fol. 1916, Wisconsin State Historical Society, Madison. United States Census, 1900. Wisconsin State Census, 1905.

Chandler, Frances Evans (Mrs. James G.) Racine, president, 1920-1922 (vice president, 1916-1920). Sources: *Racine Journal Times*, September 9, 1933, *Wisconsin Necrology*, vol. 33, pp. 34-35. *Racine Journal Times*, January 21, 1924, *Wisconsin Necrology*, vol. 21, pp. 224. "Mrs. J. G. Chandler," *Wisconsin Clubwoman*, vol. 16, September 1933, pp. 132, 168. United States Census, 1900. Wisconsin State Census, 1905.

Chynoweth, Edna Phillips (Mrs. H. W.), vice president, 1902-1904. Sources: *Madison Democrat*, October 16, 1906, *Wisconsin Necrology*, vol. 8, pp. 214-16. Graves, "Wisconsin Woman Suffrage Movement," pp. 99, 230, 337, 361. Brown, *Uncommon Lives*, p. 20. Kohler, *Story of Wisconsin Women*. Alice Bleyer to Alice Curtis, letter, February 5, 1915, Wisconsin Woman Suffrage Association Papers, Box 6, Wisconsin State Historical Society, Madison. United States Census, 1900. Wisconsin State Census, 1905.

Cole, Anne (Mrs. W. E) Fond du Lac, recording secretary, 1910-1912. Sources: *Fond du Lac Reporter*, October 1, 1929, *Wisconsin Necrology*, vol. 27, p. 56. United States Census, 1900. Wisconsin State Census, 1905.

Conley, Emma Wausau, Fond du Lac, home economics committee, member, 1908-1912, 1914-1918. Sources: Kohler, *Story of Wisconsin Women*, p. 107. *Proceedings*, 1905, p. 60; 1910, p. 78; 1914, p. 81; 1915, p. 87; 1916, p. 88; 1917, p. 79. Graves, "Wisconsin Woman Suffrage Movement," p. 282.

Connor, Mary, Windsor, district vice president, 1908-1910 and 1912-1914. Sources: *Wisconsin State Journal*, December 20, 1926, *Wisconsin Necrology*, vol. 24, pp. 114-15. Kohler, *Story of Wisconsin Women*, p. 98. *Wisconsin Alumni Directory, 1849-1919* (1921), University of Wisconsin Archives, .

Crosby, Emma (Mrs. William Howard) Racine, president, 1910-1912. Sources: *Racine Journal Times*, January 19, 1951, pp. 1-2. Dr. Willis to Crystal Eastman Benedict, letter, September 28, 1912, Ada James Papers, Box 15; Wisconsin State Historical Society, Madison.

Davis, Nellie (Mrs. Frank E.) La Crosse, district vice president, 1913-1918. Sources: *Philippi's Souvenir Directory of the City of La Crosse* (La Cross: L.P. Philippi Company, 1900, 1905, 1909). United States Census, 1900. Wisconsin State Census, 1905.

Edwards, Carrie (Mrs. Richard Henry) Oshkosh, president, 1908-1910. Sources: *Oshkosh Daily Northwestern*, February 27, 1939, p. 4. *Oshkosh Daily Northwestern*, June 2, 1943, p. 4. *Wisconsin Necrology*, vol. 49, p. 52. *Bunn's Oshkosh Directory* (Oshkosh: J. V. Bunn), 1898, p. 8, and 1908, p. 22. Sophie Gudden to Ada James, letter, October 3, 1912, Ada James Papers, Box 15, Wisconsin State Historical Society, Madison. United States Census, 1900. Wisconsin State Census, 1905.

Emerson, Della Blodgett (Mrs. C. A.) Beloit, vice president, 1904-1906. Sources: *Beloit News*, February 7, 1938, *Wisconsin Necrology*, vol. 39, pp. 190-91. *Beloit News*, February 6, 1939, *Wisconsin Necrology*, vol. 41, p. 9. United States Census, 1900. Wisconsin State Census, 1905.

Estabrook, Jennie Hodges (Mrs. C. E.) Milwaukee, auditor, 1916-1918. Sources: *Milwaukee Sentinel*, May 5, 1935, *Wisconsin Necrology*, vol. 35, p. 160. *Madison Democrat*, December 4, 1918, *Wisconsin Necrology*, vol. 17, pp. 139-40. Wisconsin Historical Society, *Dictionary of Wisconsin Biography*, p. 120. McCaul, "Wisconsin Women's War Work," p. 17. Minutes, Executive Board Meeting, April 28, 1917, Wisconsin Federation of Women's Clubs Papers, Box 1, Wisconsin State Historical Society, Madison. United States Census, 1900. Wisconsin State Census, 1905.

Frawley, Kate Coyne (Mrs. Michael S.) Eau Claire, district vice president, 1912-1914. Sources: *Eau Claire Leader*, December 15, 1925, *Wisconsin Necrology*, vol. 23, pp. 164-166. *Capital Times*, August 4, 1935, *Wisconsin Necrology*, vol. 36, p. 3. *Wisconsin Alumni Magazine*, vol. 1 (November 1899), p. 82. United States Census, 1900. Wisconsin State Census, 1905.

Gudden, Sophie (Mrs. B. C.) Oshkosh, Art Interchange and Consumers' League committees, chair, 1900-1910. Sources: *Proceedings*, 1903, pp. xv, 23-24, 37-38; 1904, p. xiv; 1905, p. xix; 1908, p. 49; 1909, pp. 35-36, 65-66; 1910, p. 71; 1911, pp. xxxiii, 23, 71; 1912, p. 76; 1913, p. 122. Kohler, *Story of Wisconsin Women*, p. 120. Publius Lawson, ed., *History of Winnebago County* (Chicago: C. F. Cooper, 1908), vol. 2, pp. 959-61. Graves, "Wisconsin Woman Suffrage Movement," pp. 143, 147. Nathan, *Epoch Making Movement*, p. 222. Various letters from Guddun, Ada James Papers, Boxes 6, 7, 15, Wisconsin State Historical Society, Madison. Various letters from Gudden to Theodora Youmans, Wisconsin Woman Suffrage Association Papers, Boxes 6 and 10, Wisconsin State Historical Society, Madison.

Hart, Jane (Mrs. Frank M.) Tomah, district vice president, 1908-1910 and 1912-1913. Sources: "Passing of a Pioneer: Mrs. F. M. Hart," *Wisconsin Clubwoman*, vol. 25, March/April 1942, p. 8. *Tomah Journal*, January 1, 1942, p. 1. Wisconsin State Census, 1905.

Harvey, Lettie Brown (Mrs. Lorenzo Dow) Menomonie, president, 1916-1918. Sources: *Wisconsin State Journal*, October 6, 1940, *Wisconsin Necrology*, vol. 43, p. 205. *Oshkosh Northwestern*, June 2, 1922, and *Fond du Lac Commonwealth*, June 2, 1922, *Wisconsin Necrology*, vol. 20, pp. 56-58. *Wisconsin Clubwoman*, vol. 23, November/December 1940, p. 11. McCaul, "Wisconsin Women's War Work," p. 17. Grace Thompson to Crystal Eastman

Benedict, letter, September 25, 1912, Ada James Papers, Box 15, Wisconsin State Historical Society, Madison. United States Census, 1900. Wisconsin State Census, 1905. Wisconsin State Census, 1915.

Hobbins, Mary (Mrs. Joseph W.) Madison, treasurer, 1912-1914. Sources: *Capital Times*, July 15, 1935, and *Wisconsin State Journal*, July 19, 1935, *Wisconsin Necrology*, vol. 35, pp. 230, 234. *Madison Democrat*, August 31, 1920, *Wisconsin Necrology*, vol. 18, p. 143. McCaul, "Wisconsin Women's War Work," p. 17. *Madison, Wisconsin City Directory* (n.p., 1917), p. 29. Graves, "Wisconsin Woman Suffrage Movement," p. 232. *Wisconsin Alumni Magazine*, vol. 3, January 1902, pp. 142-43. United States Census, 1900. Wisconsin State Census, 1905.

Holcombe, Harriett, Fond du Lac, corresponding secretary, 1904-1906. Sources: *Fond du Lac Commonwealth Reporter*, March 8, 1943, *Wisconsin Necrology*, vol. 48, pp. 237-38. United States Census, 1900. Wisconsin State Census, 1905.

Hooper, Jessie Jack (Mrs. Ben) Oshkosh, recording secretary, 1912-1914. Sources: *Oshkosh Daily Northwestern*, May 8, 1935, and *Milwaukee Sentinel*, May 19, 1935, *Wisconsin Necrology*, vol. 35, pp. 163-65. *Oshkosh Northwestern*, April 16, 1943, *Wisconsin Necrology*, vol. 48, pp. 297-98. Graves, "Wisconsin Woman Suffrage Movement," pp. 112, 142, 327. Women's Auxiliary, *Famous Wisconsin Women*, vol. 4, pp. 29-34. James, *Notable American Women*, vol. 2, pp. 215-16. Bletzinger and Short, *Wisconsin Woman*, pp. 63-65. McCaul, "Wisconsin Women's War Work" pp. 3, 36. Charlotte Witter to Theodora Youmans, letter, September 1916, Wisconsin Woman Suffrage Association Papers, Box 11, Wisconsin State Historical Society. Biography, Jessie Jack Hooper Papers, Box 21, Wisconsin State Historical Society. Wisconsin State Census, 1905.

Humphrey, Clara Dunn (Mrs. James N.) Whitewater, treasurer, 1908-1910. Sources: "Mrs. Humphrey is Named Outstanding Pioneer Clubwoman," *Whitewater Press*, April 18, 1940, *Wisconsin Necrology*, vol. 42, p. 247. *Janesville Gazette*, May 9, 1929, *Wisconsin Necrology*, vol. 26, pp. 173-74. *The Whitewater Register*, December 1, 1952, p. 1. United States Census, 1900. Wisconsin State Census, 1905.

Kimberly, Helen (Mrs. J. Alfred) Neenah, district vice president, 1900-1902. Sources: *Neenah-Menasha Daily News Times*, February 26, 1931, *Wisconsin Necrology*, vol. 29, p. 92. *Milwaukee Sentinel*, January 23, 1928, *Wisconsin Necrology*, vol. 25, pp. 110-12. *Wisconsin Clubwoman*, vol. 24, May/June 1941, pp. 10-11. United States Census, 1900. Wisconsin State Census, 1905.

Kinsman, Anna B. (Mrs. Delos O.) Whitewater; Appleton, president, 1914-1916. Sources: Wisconsin Historical Society, *Dictionary of Wisconsin Biography*, p. 207. *Who Was Who in America* (Chicago: A. N. Marquis Company, 1950), vol. 2, p. 301. *Appleton Post-Crescent*, February 21, 1915, p. 14. *Wisconsin Clubwoman*, vol. 34, March/April 1951, p. 23. Wisconsin State Census, 1905.

Knowlton, Lena (Mrs. H. M.) Waterloo, treasurer, 1910-1912. Sources: *Wisconsin State Journal*, April 2, 1942, *Wisconsin Necrology*, vol. 46, p. 194. *Capital Times*, January 13, 1937, *Wisconsin Necrology*, vol. 38, p. 43. "Second District Pioneer," *Wisconsin Clubwoman*, vol. 24, January/February 1941, p. 13. United States Census, 1900. Wisconsin State Census, 1905.

Lapham, Julia Oconomowoc, landmarks committee, chair, 1904-1908. Sources: *Oconomowoc Enterprise*, January 7, 1921, *Wisconsin Necrology*, vol. 18, pp. 228-29, 231. Increase Lapham Papers, Boxes 21 and 22, Wisconsin State Historical Society, Madison. Charlotte Reid Seybold, "The Waukesha County Historical Society," *Wisconsin Magazine of History* 32 (Winter 1948-1949): 49-50. United States Census, 1900. Wisconsin State Census, 1905.

Latimer, Mary N. (Mrs. Charles F.) Ashland, treasurer, 1902-1904. Sources: United States Census, 1900. *R. L. Polk and Company's Ashland Director* (St. Paul, MN: R. L. Polk & Company Publishers, 1897, 1904, 1909).

Magee, Adalaide (Mrs. Charles W.) Shawano, district vice president, 1908-1910 and 1916-1918. Sources: United States Census, 1900. Wisconsin State Census, 1905. Woman's Christian Temperance Union of Wisconsin, *Annual Reports*, 1902, p. 4.

Mallory, Lillian Bacon (Mrs. Rollin Bates) Milwaukee, recording secretary, 1906-1908. Sources: Gregory, *Southeastern Wisconsin*, vol. 2, pp. 394-96. United States Census, 1900. Wisconsin State Census, 1905.

Marlatt, Abby, Madison, home economics committee, member, 1910-1918. Sources: *Wisconsin State Journal,* June 24, 1943, *Wisconsin Necrology,* vol. 49, pp. 103-4. James, *Notable American Women,* vol. 2, pp. 495-97. Howes, *American Women, 1935-1940,* vol. 2, p. 565. McCaul, "Wisconsin Women's War Work," p. 17. *Proceedings,* 1916, p. 88.

Medberry, Eunice (Mrs. Chauncey J.) Fond du Lac, vice president, 1908-1910. Sources: United States Census, 1900. Wisconsin State Census, 1905. *Wright's Directory of Fond du Lac County* (Milwaukee: A. G. Wright, 1901).

Mitchell, Emma (Mrs. Alfred H.) La Crosse, vice president, 1904-1906. Sources: United States Census, 1900. Wisconsin State Census, 1905. *Philippi's Souvenir Directory,* p. 64.

Morris, Lucy (Mrs. Charles S.) Berlin, president, 1896-1898. Sources: *Milwaukee Sentinel,* May 28, 1935, *Wisconsin Necrology,* vol. 35, pp. 186-87. *Oshkosh Daily Northwestern,* February 11, 1930, *Wisconsin Necrology,* vol. 27, p. 188. "In Memory of Mrs. C. S. Morris," *Wisconsin Clubwoman,* vol. 18, June 1935, pp. 83-84. Stearns, "Mrs. Morris and the Library Movement," p. 55. Graves, "Wisconsin Woman Suffrage Movement," p. 379. Kohler, *Story of Wisconsin Women,* pp. 87-88. Bletzinger and Short, *Wisconsin Woman,* pp. 41-42. McCaul, "Wisconsin Women's War Work," pp. 7 and 38. Theodora Youmans to Crystal Eastman Benedict, letter, September 22, 1912, and Dr. Willis to Benedict, letter, September 28, 1912, Ada James Papers, Box 15, Wisconsin State Historical Society, Madison. Wisconsin State Census, 1905.

Morse, Myra (Mrs. Elmer Addison) Antigo, corresponding secretary, 1916-1918. Sources: Usher, *Wisconsin,* vol. 8, p. 2303. Wisconsin Historical Society, *Dictionary of Wisconsin Biography,* p. 260. United States Census, 1900. Wisconsin State Census, 1905.

Neville, Ella Hoes (Mrs. Arthur C.) Green Bay, president, 1898-1900. Sources: *Green Bay Gazette,* July 8, 1935, *Wisconsin Necrology,* vol. 35, pp. 224-25. *Green Bay Gazette,* May 20, 1929, *Wisconsin Necrology,* vol. 26, pp. 189-90. "Memorial to Mrs. Arthur Courtenay Neville," *Wisconsin Clubwoman,* vol. 18, September 1935, p. 123. Kohler, *Story of Wisconsin Women,* p. 91. Wisconsin State Census, 1905.

Pease, Eva May (Mrs. Earle M.) Richland Center; Grand Rapids, vice president, 1910-1912. Sources: Eva Pease to Ada James, letter, February 4, 1912, Ada James Papers, Box 7, Wisconsin State Historical Society, Madison. United States Census, 1900. Wisconsin State Census, 1905.

Pember, Ada Humphrey (Mrs. J. F.) Janesville, art committee, member, 1910-1918. Sources: *Stoughton Hub*, September 11, 1926, *Wisconsin Necrology*, vol. 24, p. 57. *Portrait and Biographical Album of Rock County, Wisconsin* (Chicago: Acme Publishing, 1889), p. 946. United States Census, 1900. Wisconsin State Census, 1905.

Perry, Helen Neely (Mrs. Ralph P.) Reedsburg, auditor, 1902-1904. Sources: *Reedsburg Times-Press*, March 9, 1944, p. 1. Holmes, *Wisconsin*, vol. 4, p. 505. United States Census, 1900. Wisconsin State Census, 1905.

Roberts, Emma Gaylord (Mrs. R. H.) Waupaca, treasurer, 1914-1916. Source: Wisconsin State Census, 1905.

Rogers, Viola (Mrs. J. H.) Portage, district vice president, 1902-1904, 1906-1908. Sources: *Portage Democrat*, December 13, 1928, *Wisconsin Necrology*, vol. 26, p. 61. *Proceedings*, 1905, p. 46. United States Census, 1900. Wisconsin State Census, 1905.

Rote, Mary K. (Mrs. Alvin F.) Monroe, vice president, 1912-1914. Sources: *Monroe Times*, February 22, 1926, *Wisconsin Necrology*, vol. 23, pp. 218-20. *Monroe Evening Times*, July 27, 1921, *Wisconsin Necrology*, vol. 19, pp. 72-74. Usher, *Wisconsin*, vol. 8, p. 2009. Mary Rote to Crystal Eastman Benedict, letter, October 1, 1912, Ada James Papers, Box 15, Wisconsin State Historical Society, Madison. United States Census, 1900. Wisconsin State Census, 1905.

Sabin, Ellen Clara, Milwaukee, committee member, 1897-1898, 1900-1912, 1914-1918. Sources: Holmes, ed. *Wisconsin*, vol. 4, pp. 47-48. Howes, *American Women, 1935-1940*, vol. 2, p. 785. Wisconsin Historical Society, *Dictionary of Wisconsin Biography*, p. 313. Women's Auxiliary, *Famous Wisconsin Women*, vol. 6, pp. 55-58. "Federation Founders," *Wisconsin Clubwoman*, vol. 23, May/June 1940, pp. 12, 33. James, *Notable American Women*, vol. 3, pp. 217-18.

Sawyer, Mary Jewell (Mrs. Edgar P.) Oshkosh, president, 1904-1906. Sources: *Oshkosh Northwestern*, November 25, 1910, *Wisconsin Necrology*, vol. 12, p. 20. *Oshkosh Northwestern*, April 23, 1927, *Wisconsin Necrology*, vol. 24, p. 195. Wisconsin State Census, 1905.

Scott, Elsie Gile (Mrs. Robert A.) La Crosse, treasurer, 1898-1900. Source: United States Census, 1900.

Shelton, Mary Howe (Mrs. Arthur W.) Rhinelander, corresponding secretary, 1914-1916. Sources: *Rhinelander Daily News*, April 25, 1923, *Wisconsin Necrology*, vol. 21, p. 78. *Proceedings*, 1899, p. 25. Reuben Thwaites, *The University of Wisconsin: Its History and Its Alumni* (Madison: J. N. Purcell, 1900), p. 790. *Wisconsin Alumni Directory*, 1849-1919 (1921), University of Wisconsin Archives. *Wright's Directory of Rhinelander and Oneida County* (Milwaukee: Wright Directory Company, 1921), pp. 35, 132. United States Census, 1900. Wisconsin State Census, 1905.

Shoemaker, Jennie Damon (Mrs. Arthur H.) Eau Claire, president, 1924-1926 (vice president, 1918-1920). Source: Usher, *Wisconsin*, vol. 7, pp. 1889-90.

Skinner, Jessie R. (Mrs. Lloyd) Madison, district vice president, 1916-1918. Source: United States Census, 1900.

Smith, Adelaide, Eau Claire, art committee, chair, 1906-1912. Source: Wisconsin State Census, 1905.

Stearns, Lutie, Milwaukee, district vice president, 1906-1908. Howes, *American Women, 1935-1940*, vol. 2, p. 860. Wisconsin State Historical Society, *Dictionary of Wisconsin Biography*, p. 337. Brown, *Uncommon Lives*, pp. 44-45. "Federation Founders," *Wisconsin Clubwoman*, vol. 23, May/June 1940, pp. 13, 33. Stearns, "Mrs. Morris and the Library Movement," p. 55. Kohler, *Story of Wisconsin Women*, pp. 88-89. Graves, "Wisconsin Woman Suffrage Movement," pp. 112, 127, 147, 224-30. James, *Notable American Women*, vol. 3, pp. 353-54. Stearns, "My Seventy-Five Years, Part I," pp. 211-18. Stearns, "My Seventy-Five Years, Part II," pp. 282-87. Stearns, "My Seventy-Five Years, Part III," pp. 97-105.

Strathearn, Sophie (Mrs. John A.) Kaukauna; Manitowoc, president, 1912-1914. Sources: Howes, *American Women*, vol. 2, p. 875. "Forty-Two Years . . . And More," pp. 19, 30-31. *Manitowoc Herald-Times*, August 24, 1948, p. 2. Graves, "Wisconsin Woman Suffrage Movement," p. 378. Sophie Strathearn to "Comrade" James, letter February 13, 1911, Ada James Papers, Box 5, Wisconsin State Historical Society, Madison. United States Census, 1900. Wisconsin State Census, 1905.

Swart, Rose, Oshkosh, committee member, 1900-1918. Sources: *Oshkosh Northwestern*, December 21, 1939, *Wisconsin Necrology*, vol. 42, p. 48. Graves, "Wisconsin Woman Suffrage Movement," p. 379. Kohler, *Story of Wisconsin Women*, p. 113. Wisconsin State Census, 1905.

Tanberg, Ella (Mrs. Albert E.) Janesville; Monroe, district vice president, 1901-1904. Source: United States Census, 1900.

Teetshorn, Kate Somerville (Mrs. Frank Edson) Green Bay, recording secretary, 1902-1904. Sources: *Green Bay Gazette*, June 27, 1921, *Wisconsin Necrology*, vol. 19, p. 63. Wisconsin Census, 1905.

Tichenor, Caroline (Mrs. Willard H.) Waupun, correspondence secretary, 1906-1908. Sources: *Waupun Leader*, October 20, 1909, p. 1. United States Census, 1900. Wisconsin State Census, 1905.

Trevitt, Dr. Margaret (Mrs. A. W.) Wausau, vice president, 1906-1908. Sources: *Wausau Daily Record-Herald*, March 11, 1937, *Wisconsin Necrology*, vol. 38, pp. 119-20. *Wausau Daily Record-Herald*, December 7, 1925, p. 1. *Wausau Pilot*, December 10, 1925, p. 1. Wisconsin State Census, 1905.

Van Ostrand, Mattie Culver (Mrs. Edwin H.) Antigo; Madison, landmarks committee, chair, 1912-1916. Sources: *Antigo Journal*, October 31, 1928, *Wisconsin Necrology*, vol. 26, p. 39. Quaife, *Wisconsin*, vol. 1, pp. 386-89. Wisconsin State Census, 1905.

Wadsworth, Anna (Mrs. J. S.) River Falls, corresponding secretary, 1912-1914. Sources: *River Falls Morning Sentinel*, June 11, 1942, *Wisconsin Necrology*, vol. 47, pp. 58-59. United State Census, 1900.

Wheeler, Mabel E. (Mrs. Lyman G.) Wauwatosa, corresponding secretary, 1910-1912. Sources: *Milwaukee Journal*, June 6, 1932, *Wisconsin Necrology*, vol. 31, p. 54. United States Census, 1900. Wisconsin State Census, 1905.

Whyte, Hannah Griffith (Mrs. David G.) La Crosse, corresponding secretary, 1900-1902. Sources: United States Census, 1900. Wisconsin State Census, 1905.

Witter, Charlotte G. (Mrs. Isaac P.) Grand Rapids, district vice president, 1910-1912. Sources: *Wisconsin Rapids Tribune*, September 26, 1942, *Wisconsin Necrology*, vol. 47, pp. 209-10. Holmes, *Wisconsin*, vol. 4, pp. 225-28. *The Wisconsin Citizen*, vol. 28, December 1915, p. 6. Graves, "Wisconsin Woman Suffrage Movement," p. 378. McCaul, "Wisconsin Women's War Work," p. 38. Wisconsin State Census, 1905.

Wright, Ione Turner (Mrs. Walter H.) Wauwatosa, district vice president, 1898-1900. Sources: United States Census, 1900. Wisconsin State Census, 1905.

Youmans, Theodora (Mrs. Henry M.) Waukesha, president, 1900-1902. Sources: *Waukesha Daily Freeman*, August 17, 1932, *Wisconsin Necrology*, vol. 31, pp. 134-36. *Waukesha Daily Freeman*, January 21, 1931, *Wisconsin Necrology*, vol. 29, pp. 65-67. Seybold, "Waukesha County Historical Society," pp. 49-50. Women's Auxiliary, *Famous Wisconsin Women*, vol. 2 pp. 13-16. Graves, "Wisconsin Woman Suffrage Movement," pp. 142, 146, 195, 246, 360, 285. United States Census, 1900. Wisconsin State Census, 1905. Letters, Youmans to Ada James, and Youmans to Crystal Eastman Benedict, Ada James Papers, Boxes 6, 7, 15; Wisconsin State Historical Society, Madison.

Notes

EDITOR'S INTRODUCTION

1. Edward T. James, Janet Wilson James, and Paul S. Boyer. eds. *Notable American Women, 1607-1950: A Biographical Dictionary*, 3 vols. (Cambridge: Harvard University Press, 1971); Barbara Sicherman and Carol Hurd Green, eds., *Notable American Women, the Modern Period: A Biographical Dictionary* (Cambridge: Harvard University Press, 1980).
2. New York: R.R. Bowker, 1979.

CHAPTER ONE

1. Sophonisba P. Breckinridge, *Women in the Twentieth Century: A Study of Their Political, Social and Economic Activities* (New York: McGraw-Hill, Inc., 1933), p. 30; General Federation of Women's Clubs, *Proceedings of the Twelfth Biennial Convention*, 1914.
2. Jane Cunningham Croly, *The History of the Woman's Club Movement in America* (New York: Henry G. Allen, 1898); Mary I. Wood, *The History of the General Federation of Women's Clubs for the First Twenty-Two Years of its Organization* (New York: General Federation of Women's Clubs, 1912); Mildred White Wells, *Unity in Diversity: The History of the General Federation of Women's Clubs* (Washington, D.C.: General Federation of Women's Clubs, 1953). Also useful is *Annals of the American Academy of Political and Social Science*, vol. 28, no. 2 (September 1906), which contains a series of articles about the woman's club movement by leading participants.
3. Karen J. Blair, *The Clubwoman as Feminist: True Womanhood Redefined, 1868-1914* (New York: Holmes & Meier, 1980), p. 4.
4. Croly, *History*, p. 24. For accounts of the beginnings of Sorosis, see Croly, pp. 15-23 and Blair, *Clubwoman*, pp. 20-21.
5. Croly, *History*, pp. 18, 25; Blair, *Clubwoman*, pp. 21-22.
6. Blair, *Clubwoman*, pp. 25-27.
7. Croly, *History*, p. 31.
8. Blair, *Clubwoman*, pp. 28-29.
9. Ibid., pp. 22-23; Croly, *History*, p. 18.

10. Croly, *History*, pp. 36-37; Blair, *Clubwoman*, pp. 31-33.
11. Croly, *History*, pp. 42-43.
12. Breckinridge, *Women in Twentieth Century*, p. 17, and Mary Ritter Beard, *Woman's Work in Municipalities* (New York: D. Appleton, 1915), pp. 221-23, 260. A useful discussion of the impact of technological change on the domestic life of middle class women during the latter half of the nineteenth century is found in Sheila Rothman, *Woman's Proper Place: A History of Changing Ideals and Practices, 1870 to the Present* (New York: Basic Books, 1978), pp. 13-21.
13. Blair, *Clubwoman*, pp. 59-61, 118. According to Blair, education raised women's expectations, which were then disappointed by the realities of domestic life.
14. Croly, *History*, p. 1167.
15. Wisconsin State Federation of Women's Clubs, *Proceedings of the Annual Convention*, 1899, p. 24.
16. Blair, *Clubwoman*, p. 69; Nelson A. Ault, "The Earnest Ladies: The Walla Walla Woman's Club and the Equal Suffrage League of 1886-1889," *Pacific Northwest Quarterly* 42 (April 1951): 127.
17. Minutes, 1894-1906, Kaukauna Woman's Club Records, 1894-1977, Box 1, especially pp. 90-92, 141-328, Wisconsin State Historical Society—Green Bay Area Research Center.
18. Wisconsin Federation of Women's Clubs, *Proceedings of the Twelfth Annual Convention* (1908), p. 28.
19. Croly, *History*, p. 1151; Wisconsin Federation of Women's Clubs, *Proceedings of the First Annual Convention* (1897), p. 71.
20. Wisconsin Federation of Women's Clubs, *Proceedings of the Annual Conventions*, 1897, p. 17; 1898, p. 19; 1899, p. 15; 1900, pp. 16, 31, 44, 51-52; Croly, *History*, pp. 1164-67.
21. Croly, *History*, pp. 78-79. Also Beard, *Woman's Work*, p. 199.
22. Minutes, 1900-1911, River Falls Improvement League Records, Box 1, volumes 1 and 2, Wisconsin State Historical Society—River Falls Area Research Center.
23. This summary is based on Beard, *Woman's Work*, WFWC convention reports, and *Annals of the American Academy*. On the importance of women's clubs in reshaping the configuration of governmental responsibilities, see Beard, pp. 45-46, 221; Breckinridge, *Women in Twentieth Century*, p. 93; Blair, *Clubwoman*, p. 93.
24. Blair, *Clubwoman*, especially pp. 58, 66-69. See also Celia Burliegh (member of Sorosis), cited in Croly, *History*, p. 27; Anna McMahan (member of Friends in Council, Quincy, Illinois), 1892, cited p. 59, and Mary Channing Wistor (member of the Civic Club of Philadelphia), 1895, cited p. 78.
25. Blair, *Clubwoman*, pp. 93-95; Breckinridge, *Women in Twentieth Century*, pp. 14, 17.
26. Figures from Wells, *Unity*, pp. 471-73; Breckinridge, *Women in Twentieth Century*, pp. 19, 30; *Annals of the American Academy*, p. 2; General Federation of Women's Clubs, *Proceedings of the Biennial Conventions*.

27. Breckinridge, *Women in Twentieth Century*, pp. 17-19; Wells, *Unity*, pp. 28-39, 165-66.

28. Forestry may seem a strange interest for clubwomen. The committee was devoted to agitating for the protection of forests and trees, for both their economic and aesthetic value. The Wisconsin Federation also had a forestry committee.

29. Lists of standing committees were taken from General Federation of Women's Clubs, *Proceedings of the Biennial Conventions*. See also Wells, *Unity*, pp. 165-66.

30. Breckinridge, *Women in Twentieth Century*, pp. 19, 21; Wells, *Unity*, pp. 199-201, 227.

31. Blair, *Clubwoman*, p. 97; *Annals of the American Academy*, pp. 4, 95; Wells, *Unity*, pp. 57, 60.

32. Wells, *Unity*, Chapter 11.

33. Ibid., p. 37; Blair, *Clubwoman*, pp. 96-97.

34. Wells, *Unity*, Chapter 11; *Annals of the American Academy*, throughout.

35. Blair, *Clubwoman*, pp. 108-9; Gerda Lerner, "Community Work of Black Club Women," in Gerda Lerner, *The Majority Finds Its Past* (New York: Oxford University Press, 1979), p. 87.

36. Lerner, "Community Work."

37. The General Federation's late endorsement of suffrage does not describe fully the relationship of the woman's club movement to women's demand for the vote. Suffragists frequently joined women's clubs and often were leaders in the General Federation. And women's clubs may have nurtured the development of suffrage sentiment. The history of the Walla Walla (Washington) Woman's Club suggests a positive connection between women's clubs and suffrage. In 1886, several women in Walla Walla organized a self-improvement club, devoted to discussion of literature, religion, children, the home, and education. These clubwomen also frequently discussed subjects explicitly related to women, including suffrage. The Walla Walla club was short-lived; formed in 1886, club meetings and membership began to fall off by the end of 1887. The club disbanded by the beginning of 1889, but many of its former members helped to organize the Equal Suffrage League in April 1889, whose purpose was to participate in the struggle for woman suffrage in Washington. It is not clear whether these women supported suffrage when they joined the Walla Walla Women's Club, so that the specific connection between suffrage support and women's clubs remains undefined. On the history of the Walla Walla clubs, see Ault, "Earnest Ladies." And on prosuffragist members of clubs and the GFWC, see Blair, *Clubwoman*, pp. 27, 34, 70, 111-14.

38. Beard, *Woman's Work*, p. 318.

39. Ibid., especially pp. 38, 70, 84.

40. Ibid., especially pp. 221-23, 260.

41. Breckinridge, *Women in Twentieth Century*, especially pp. 17, 26, 33. During the first decade of the twentieth century, the National Education Association inaugurated the Education Department of National Organizations of Women. Representatives from the GFWC, the National Council of Jewish Women, and

the Association of Collegiate Alumnae were members of this department. Several national women's organizations were affiliated with GFWC.

42. Ibid., pp. 11-12, 28.
43. Ibid., pp. 17-23, 28-32, 39-40, 51-53.
44. William O'Neill, *Everyone Was Brave: The Rise and Fall of Feminism in America* (Chicago: Quadrangle Books, 1969), especially Chapters 3, 5, 10.
45. Jill Conway, "Women Reformers and American Culture, 1870-1930," in Jean E. Friedman and William G. Shade, eds., *Our American Sisters: Women in American Life and Thought* (Boston: Allyn and Bacon, 1973), pp. 301-12.
46. Daniel Scott Smith, "Family Limitation, Sexual Control and Domestic Feminism in Victorian America," in Nancy F. Cott and Elizabeth H. Pleck, eds., *A Heritage of Her Own* (New York: Simon and Schuster, 1979), p. 236.
47. Blair, *Clubwoman*, especially pp. 27, 118. Leaders in the Wisconsin Federation of Women's Clubs often railed against the greedy immorality of the competitive world of business, contrasting it with the gentler morality usually associated with feminine sensibilities. For example, in 1900, President Ella Neville said:

> The question of capital and labor is today one of the most perplexing which is waiting for solution, and one to which women's clubs should attend with "a hearing ear and a seeing eye." Self assertion seems to be the essence of the cosmic process "to survive, to survive with ever increasing power, to survive no matter who goes under," this is the way in which evolution explains the process by which the world has reached its present culmination of material power. Applied to social conditions this assertive effort had made political economists believe the law of supply and demand to be as unchangeable as the law of gravitation or the attraction of cohesion. Meanwhile the "almighty dollar has acquired a momentum and brilliancy that have lifted it to the place of the sun in the heavens," where its dazzling rays have so bewildered the beholder that he looks at nothing else but stretches both his hands to bring it within his grasp, crushing tender women and helpless children in his efforts to make it his.

Neville then discussed the WFWC's new plans to "assist in solving the question of supply and demand." Evidently, Neville did not believe such economic laws were as immutable as the experts would have led her to believe. For this citation, and other similar examples, see Wisconsin Federation of Women's Clubs, *Proceedings of the Annual Conventions*, 1900, p. 6; 1905, p. 9; 1907, p. 6; 1914, p. 61.

48. Blair, *Clubwoman*, especially pp. 3-5, 119.
49. Ibid.
50. Ibid., pp. 98-103.
51. Estelle Freedman, "Separatism as Strategy: Female Institution Building and American Feminism, 1870-1930," *Feminist Studies* 5 (Fall 1979): 512-28.

52. Ibid., p. 513. Examples of such cross-cultural studies can be found in Michelle Rosaldo and Louise Lamphere, eds., *Woman, Culture and Society* (Stanford: Stanford University Press, 1974), and Rayna R. Reiter, ed., *Toward an Anthropology of Women* (New York: Monthly Review Press, 1975).
53. Ruth Bordin, *Woman and Temperance: The Quest for Power and Liberty, 1873-1900* (Philadelphia: Temple University Press, 1981), p. 94.
54. See ibid.; Barbara Leslie Epstein, *The Politics of Domesticity: Women, Evangelism and Temperance in Nineteenth Century America* (Middletown, Connecticut: Wesleyan University Press, 1981).
55. Epstein, *Domesticity*, Chapter 5.
56. Beard, p. 318.

CHAPTER TWO

1. William Chafe, *The American Woman: Her Changing Social, Economic and Political Roles, 1920-1970* (New York: Oxford University Press, 1972), p. 36.
2. Information on the formation of the Wisconsin Federation of Women's Clubs is from General Federation of Women's Clubs, *Proceedings of the Third Biennial Convention* (Louisville: John P. Morton, 1896), pp. 110-11, and Wisconsin Federation of Women's Clubs, *Proceedings of the First Annual Convention* (Berlin, Wisconsin: Geo. C. Hicks, 1897) pp. v-vi, 11-12. The reports of the annual conventions, a major source for this chapter, are hereinafter cited as *Proceedings*.
3. The annual reports of the corresponding secretaries contain estimates of WFWC membership. See *Proceedings*, 1897, p. 14; 1899, p.10; 1900, p.12; 1901, p. 13; 1902, p. 17; 1903, p. 13; 1904, p. 13; 1905, p. 15; 1906, p. 17; 1908, p. 14; 1909, p. 7; 1910, p. 10; 1911, p. 15; 1912, p. 10; 1913, p. 21; 1914, p. 58; 1915, p. 58; 1916, p. 10; 1917, p. 65.
4. The education committee was from its beginning a very active force in the WFWC, and it remained so throughout the first decades of the twentieth century. The committee supported a variety of Progressive school reforms and improvements, such as kindergartens, industrial arts and home economics courses, summer schools, special education for mentally and physically handicapped children, physical plant improvements like playgrounds and better ventilation in schools, free lunches and medical examinations for poor children, and higher salaries for teachers. In 1904 the WFWC also inaugurated a loan fund for the higher education of women, administered by a special standing committee.

Libraries also were among Wisconsin clubwomen's favorite projects. The library committee, which helped clubwomen establish and support community libraries and collected its own traveling library for club use, gradually lost some of its purpose as the state's Free Library Commission became increasingly successful in the promotion of public libraries. Clubwomen were strong supporters of the Library Commission and maintained numerous connections with it, eventually merging the library committee with a department of the Free Library Commission.

The art interchange committee expressed Federation members' belief in the power of art to develop a love of beauty. The committee argued that if this aesthetic appreciation took hold among the populace generally, it could bring about social and ethical regeneration. Wisconsin clubwomen sponsored community art exhibits and placed artworks in classrooms.

5. The town and village improvement committee, organized in 1898 and later renamed the civics committee, first represented this broadened interest. A wide range of activity came within its purview—all projects that in any way increased the efficiency, beauty, or healthfulness of Wisconsin cities and towns. With suggestions of work clubwomen could undertake, and advice aimed at ensuring success, this committee nurtured and gently directed clubwomen's growing interest in public, community activity.

6. In 1903, the landmarks committee began an active and successful career. The committee urged clubwomen to see to the preservation of local historical and archaeological sites and to collect historically interesting objects and information from local residents who had been pioneers. It supplied information to clubs about the historical sites in their localities that needed attention. The landmarks committee was especially concerned with the protection of burial and effigy mounds and other archaeological remains left by Wisconsin Native Americans. It urged the legislature, with some success, to buy and maintain these sites, and pressured private owners to protect them. In 1911, the committee purchased for the Federation the site of the territorial legislature in Belmont, erecting there a surrounding fence and commemorative marker.

7. The forestry committee, organized in 1904 and later renamed the conservation committee, aroused a surprising degree of interest among clubwomen. The committee pressed the issue of conservation of natural resources, and urged clubwomen to develop an appreciation for the beauty of nature. Committee members appealed to clubwomen's belief in both the thriftiness of the good housewife who uses resources efficiently and the inherently superior aesthetic sensibility of women. The forestry committee successfully organized a campaign to have certain forest areas set aside as state parks.

8. See, for example, *Proceedings*, 1898, pp. 49-51; 1899, pp. 36-37, 39; 1914, pp. 58-60, 62. The minutes of the River Falls Tuesday Club, a member of the WFWC, reveal this process from the viewpoint of the clubs. Minutes from club meetings between 1905 and 1915 mention letters from the forestry, landmarks, loan fund, industrial and social conditions, civics, and home economics committees. Sometimes the club responded as requested by these letters; sometimes club members voted to "lay them on the table," evidently ignoring them. See "Minute Books," River Falls Tuesday Club Papers, volumes 1, 2, and 3, Wisconsin State Historical Society—River Falls Area Research Center.

9. See, for example, *Proceedings*, 1901, p. 42; 1902, pp. 39-40; 1907, p. 50.

10. In 1900, several WFWC leaders were instrumental in organizing a Wisconsin State Consumers' League. Information on the Consumers' League committee is

found in its annual reports in the convention proceedings. See especially *Proceedings*, 1899, pp. viii-ix, 36-37; 1900, pp. 47, 49-50; 1907, p. 48; 1908, pp. 50-51; 1909, p. 65.

11. *Proceedings*, 1907, p. 6.

12. *Proceedings*, 1911, p. 84.

13. *Proceedings*, 1897, p. 48.

14. *Proceedings*, 1898, p. 8; 1901, p. 2.

15. *Proceedings*, 1901, pp. xii-xiii; 1903, p. 42; 1904, p. 21. Because of the problems WFWC leaders encountered in raising the money, the $5,000 Kimberly offered for an educational loan fund was used for the domestic science fund instead. Kimberly later gave $500 toward an educational load fund.

16. *Proceedings*, 1910, p. xxix; 1911, pp. 5, 81; 1913, p. 61.

17. *Proceedings*, 1901, p. 52.

18. *Proceedings*, 1916, p. 87. See also 1910, p. xxix.

19. *Proceedings*, 1908, pp. 53-56, 72. The civics committee report was devoted to community projects for the prevention and control of tuberculosis, and convention delegates passed a resolution urging installation of public drinking fountains to replace shared drinking cups.

20. *Proceedings*, 1909, p. 83.

21. *Proceedings*, 1910, pp. 88-91.

22. *Proceedings*, 1914, pp. 18, 30; 1915, pp. 39-40.

23. Alice Louise McCaul, "Wisconsin Women's War Work" (bachelor's thesis, University of Wisconsin, 1930), pp. 7, 12-18; *Proceedings*, 1917, p. 50.

24. *Proceedings*, 1917, p. 51. See also *The Wisconsin Clubwoman*, vol. 23, November/December 1940, p. 11, Wisconsin Federation of Women's Clubs, "Papers," Box 1, Convention Minutes—January 29, 1919, Wisconsin Historical Society: Archives and Manuscripts Department, Madison.

25. McCaul, "Women's War Work," pp. 9-10, 44-82; *Proceedings*, 1917, especially pp. 46-52, 80-81.

26. *Proceedings*, 1917, p. 46.

27. In 1905, district vice president Augusta Bolds scolded unnamed Federation leaders for what she saw as jealous protection of statewide leaders' power. She defended district vice presidents, arguing that they could lead the clubs of their districts because club members knew them. Federation officers, often distant and unfamiliar, sometimes were less effective; Bolds observed of some clubs, "a stranger they will not follow." Bolds's outspoken criticism is all the more significant because clubwomen were almost always mild in their criticisms of one another at public conventions. *Proceedings*, 1905, p. 45.

28. In 1912, President Crosby addressed this confusion. She explained to convention delegates that the "district auxiliaries" were part of, not separate from, the state organization and hence they should be—and were—loyal to the state Federation and its goals. *Proceedings*, 1912, pp. 8-9.

29. *Proceedings*, 1903, p. 32; 1905, p. 8; 1914, p. 80; 1916, p. 50.

30. For example, *Proceedings*, 1908, pp. 53-54; 1914, pp. 63-64; 1915, pp. 86, 88, 92; 1916, p. 66. Sometimes the WFWC even organized new committees at the urging of the GFWC, and changed the names of old committees to correspond with GFWC committees.
31. *Proceedings*, 1913, pp. 24-25.
32. *Proceedings*, 1902, p. 10; 1904, pp. 56-57.
33. *Proceedings*, 1905, p. 53; 1911, pp. 4, 7-8, 10, 14; 1912, pp. xxviii, 7; 1913, p. 59; 1914, p. 49.
34. *Proceedings*, 1905, p. 45; 1912, p. 83.
35. For example, *Proceedings*, 1904, p. 16; 1906, p. 19.
36. *Proceedings*, 1902, pp. 7-8; 1904, p. 59.
37. *Proceedings*, 1908, pp. 8, 13-14.
38. *Proceedings*, 1910, pp. xxi, xxiv-xxv; 1912, p. 17; 1915, pp. 81-85; 1916, pp. 53, 67, 80, 96.
39. *Proceedings*, 1916, p. 68.
40. Ibid., p. 10.
41. *Proceedings*, 1897, p. 5.
42. For example, *Proceedings*, 1911, pp. 10-13.
43. Examples can be found in *Proceedings*, 1908, p. 1; 1909, pp. 1-2; 1913, pp. 11-14; 1914, p. 38. See also 1916, p. 53, for evidence that good feelings were not always maintained.
44. *Proceedings*, 1915, p. 43.
45. *Proceedings*, 1905, p. 9.
46. See *Proceedings*, 1906, p. xvi; 1910, p. xxviii; 1912, pp. xxvii, xxix; 1914, pp. 31, 62-63.
47. *Proceedings*, 1898, p. 10.
48. *Proceedings*, 1912, p. 3. Bolds made this speech at the convention that endorsed woman suffrage. She spoke with the belief that Wisconsin women would soon win the vote, and she urged clubwomen to recognize that fulfilling their responsibilities meant participating in the world of politics. She knew she was treading on controversial ground. She ended her address noting that she would "Hail the day when neither a mouse nor the shadow of coming citizenship shall appall us or make us afraid."
49. See *Proceedings*, 1906, p. 10; 1910, p. 8; 1912, p. 98.
50. *Proceedings*, 1897, p. 11.
51. *Proceedings*, 1902, p. 30. Sabin had something of a vested interest in her audience's acceptance of such ideas. She was, at the time, encouraging her listeners to donate to a fund being raised for the chair of domestic science at her college. Still, Sabin seems to have held some fairly traditional ideas about the place of most women.
52. *Proceedings*, 1897, p. 71.
53. *Proceedings*, 1900, p. 7.
54. *Proceedings*, 1915, pp. 50-51.
55. *Proceedings*, 1897, pp. 36, 44; 1898, p. 36.

56. Sabin was by no means the only single career woman to assert that homemaking was woman's best and truest role. See also, for example, *Proceedings*, 1897, p. 65.
57. *Proceedings*, 1897, p. 7, 88-89; 1915, p. 44.
58. *Proceedings*, 1908, p. 5.
59. *Proceedings*, 1902, p. 2.
60. *Proceedings*, 1897, pp. 88-89.
61. *Proceedings*, 1905, p. 10; see also 1900, p. 5.
62. *Proceedings*, 1899, p. 6; 1906, p. 8.
63. For example, *Proceedings*, 1909, p. 84.
64. *Proceedings*, 1897, p. 72.
65. *Proceedings*, 1905, pp. 9-10.
66. For example, *Proceedings*, 1899, pp. 5-6.
67. *Proceedings*, 1897, p. 66; 1899, p. 23.
68. To some extent, clubwomen's defensive and cautious tone may have been a public relations device to ensure that criticism of their activities remain low. It is difficult to assess just how much placating of possible critics, how much posturing, is going on, and how much of it clubwomen believed.
69. *Proceedings*, 1898, pp. 39, 43.
70. *Proceedings*, 1900, p. x; 1902, pp. 58-59.
71. *Proceedings*, 1902, p. 9.
72. Ibid., p. 5. Attempts to maintain a civil service reform committee foundered in large part on Wisconsin clubwomen's fear of the explicitly political. Civil service reform was a compelling issue to several General Federation leaders; as staunch progressives, problems of patronage and dishonesty in government appalled them. At the immediate urging of the WFWC president in 1904, the Wisconsin Federation established the civil service reform committee. Unable to arouse enough interest among clubwomen to sustain its existence, it disappeared three years later. Reorganized in 1911, the civil service reform committee vanished again in 1914. Youmans was its first chair and she blamed clubwomen's disinterest in part on the relatively advanced state of Wisconsin's civil service laws. She also hinted at the problem posed by its highly political nature. Indeed women, making such a vast criticism of the way male politicians had organized governmental administration, must have seemed a direct attack on the male's public prerogatives, especially to clubwomen who still retained a vision of women's own private sphere. See *Proceedings*, 1906, p. 73; 1907, p. 6.
73. *Proceedings*, 1906, pp. 74-75.
74. *Proceedings*, 1907, pp. xvii, 6, 71-72.
75. *Proceedings*, 1909, p. 83.
76. *Proceedings*, 1910, p. 8.
77. *Proceedings*, 1911, p. 6.
78. Ibid., pp. xxxii-xxxiv.
79. *Proceedings*, 1912, pp. xxx-xxxviii; Lawrence Graves, "The Wisconsin Woman Suffrage Movement, 1846-1920" (Ph.D. dissertation, University of Wisconsin,

1954), p. 195. The policy committee never prevented resolutions from presentation to the full body of delegates, but its recommendations were generally accepted. Due to the unavoidable absence of several leaders from the convention, substitutions had to be made on the policy committee just before it made its judgments on the proposed resolutions. The original policy committee included Lucy Morris, and evidence indicates that a majority of this original committee was prosuffrage. Last-minute substitutions changed the character of the committee.

80. See, for example, *Proceedings*, 1915, p. 97. See also Theodora Youmans to Ada James, undated letter, Ada James Papers, Box 7, Wisconsin State Historical Society: Archives and Manuscripts Department, Madison. Youmans lamented to James that despite the convention's endorsement of suffrage, the legislative committee did nothing at all in response to prosuffrage measures.

81. *Proceedings*, 1914, p. 22; 1915, pp. 29, 35. Suffrage supporters were permitted to make prosuffrage announcements from the convention platform. And the *Wisconsin Citizen*, vol. 27, November 1914, p. 2, published by the Wisconsin Woman Suffrage Association, noted approvingly "that the club conventions are coming more and more to have the same personnel."

82. *Proceedings*, 1912, p. 84. See also, 1916, pp. 85-86.

83. *Proceedings*, 1913, pp. 16-17. Originally the political science subcommittee was part of the education committee, probably reflecting the strategy of having clubwomen study a subject, with the expectation that action would follow.

84. One particularly eloquent statement of this belief is found in President Sawyer's 1905 presidential address. *Proceedings*, 1905, pp. 6-7.

85. *Proceedings*, 1901, p. 3.

86. *Proceedings*, 1897, pp. 36, 39; 1898, p. 19; 1899, p. 43; 1900, pp. x, 32, 44; 1904, p. 54; 1905, p. 33; 1907, p. 35; 1909, pp. 82-83; 1910, pp. xxix-xxx, 22; 1911, p. 70; 1912, pp. 40-41; 1914, pp. 30-31, 59, 98, 102; 1915, p. 92.

87. For example, *Proceedings*, 1902, p. xiv; 1911, p. xxv; 1917, p. 33.

88. Examples may be found in *Proceedings*, 1897, p. 51; 1898, pp. 28, 31, 34; 1899, p. 13; 1900, pp. x, 29; 1903, pp. 29, 41, 55; 1904, p. 54; 1907, pp. 16, 35; 1910, pp. 39, 45-46; 1914, pp. 67-68; 1915, p. 30; 1916, pp. 116, 142; 1917, pp. 112, 128, 137.

89. *Proceedings*, 1897, pp. 79-80; 1898, p. xi; 1903, p. xiii; 1904, p. 67; 1905, pp. 13, 46; 1907, p. 3; 1912, p. xxxi; 1915, p. 80.

90. *Proceedings*, 1903, pp. xii, 17; 1904, p. xvii; 1911, pp. 4-5; 1915, p. 46.

91. *Proceedings*, 1898, pp. 2, 39-40. The WFWC organized a Congress of Women at the Wisconsin semicentennial celebration. And a member of the education committee initiated at the Chippewa Falls Fair the erection of a "social pavilion." The WFWC and other women's organizations, as well as representatives of the state library commission and teachers' organizations used the pavilion to make the public more familiar with their aims and ideas. According to the education committee, the pavilion also was a pleasant place where tired mothers could bring their families to eat and rest, a concern akin to the modern feminist attention to

child care facilities at public events. Both represent a sensitivity to the fact that caring for children is nonstop work.

92. *Proceedings*, 1904, p. 67; 1905, p. 46; 1909, p. xxiv; 1911, pp. 4-5; 1915, pp. 39-40, 46, 80. On WFWC concerns about morally offensive entertainment, see, for example, *Proceedings*, 1913, pp. 49, 56; 1914, pp. 30-31, 44, 63; 1915, pp. 55, 91.

93. *Proceedings*, 1898, p. 28; 1901, p. xi; 1902, pp. xiii, 57-58; 1903, p. xv; 1904, pp. xiv, 67; 1905, pp. 46, 49; 1907, pp. 3, 60, 63; 1909, pp. xii, xiv, 63, 65; 1910, pp. xxii, xxviii; 1911, pp. xxxi-xxxii, xxviii, 4-5; 1912, p. xxiii; 1913, pp. 2, 17; 1914, pp. 19, 26, 43, 69; 1915, pp. 37, 46; 1917, p. 49.

94. The Federation also responded positively to invitations to the National Conservation Congress and Good Roads Congress. *Proceedings*, 1907, p. 3; 1912, p. 8; 1913, pp. 2, 17; 1914, pp. 16, 43; 1915, pp. 27, 34, 46; 1916, p. 92; 1917, p. 39.

95. At first, the WFWC provided the Library Commission with "unofficial support." The connection became official when the Library Commission took over the Federation's traveling library. Lucy Morris was serving on the library committee when this official link was formed. Urging clubwomen to accept the Commission's offer, she implied that she saw value in formal connections with other organizations: "From the very first, I cherished the hope of such an alliance as the one offered to us." See *Proceedings*, 1905, pp. 65-66, for Morris's discussion. On the WFWC and the Free Library Commission generally, see *Proceedings*, 1899, pp. 5, 34; 1905, pp. xix-xx, 65-66; 1907, p. 6. On the suggestions of the town improvement committee, see *Proceedings*, 1899, pp. 36-37; 1900, p. 43.

96. *Proceedings*, 1906, p. xv; 1908, p. 7; 1916, p. 107.

97. *Proceedings*, 1900, pp. 49-51; 1905, pp. iv, 46; 1908, p. 7; 1913, p. 7; 1915, p. 41.

98. *Proceedings*, 1905, p. xix; 1914, p. 62.

CHAPTER THREE

1. On the Board of Control, see *The Blue Book of the State of Wisconsin* (Milwaukee: Henry Gugler, 1897), p. 449.

2. Sometimes they even bypassed official authority by making changes on their own, for example, making small improvements in the school building or grounds or additions to classroom supplies. See *Proceedings*, 1897, pp. 21, 28, 31-33.

3. *Proceedings*, 1897, pp. 31, 38-39.

4. Ibid., p. 39.

5. Ibid., pp. 31, 38.

6. Ibid., pp. 39, 41. Hall added a class-based justification for putting women on the Board of Control. She made a special plea for "ladies of wealth, culture, and refinement who are confined [in state institutions] day after day in the same room or ward with the lowest element of our foreign-born population, ignorant and

filthy, many of them unable to speak the English language. Such as these are the constant companions of our dear ones day and night, for they sleep in the same rooms. Is it any wonder with such an environment that they do not recover their reason?" Hall believed that women members of the Board of Control would "advocate and insist upon classifying of patients and the better class or their friends the privilege of using their own funds to buy for them a little more privacy in their misfortunes" (pp. 40-41). Other clubwomen expressed similar class and ethnic prejudice, but usually not so virulently as this. And overall, their arguments for appointing women to the Board of Control centered much more on the value of supposedly feminine traits than the special protection due to upper-class ladies.

7. Ibid., pp. 39, 41.
8. *Proceedings*, 1898, p. 41.
9. Ibid., pp. 41-42.
10. Ibid., p. 42.
11. Ibid., pp. 41-42. The committee used the phrase "true woman."
12. Although as individuals many clubwomen may have struggled with self-confidence, they had a very high, at times self-righteous, opinion of clubwomen as a group.
13. *In Assembly: Journals of the Proceedings of the Forty-Fourth Session of the Wisconsin Legislature* (Madison: Democrat Printing Company, 1899), pp. 190, 1105. Hereafter cited as *Assembly Journal*.
14. On McGrath, see *Blue Book*, p. 763.
15. *Proceedings*, 1899, p. 27; *Assembly Journal*, 1899, pp. 531, 690. It is possible that some clubs sent letters that were not introduced into the Assembly's record, but if so, none was reported at the 1899 convention. Since clubs frequently reported activity of this sort, it suggests that Federation clubs did not collectively place this kind of pressure on their state representatives.
16. Ibid., p. 4. There are no records of Assembly committee hearings, and nothing to indicate the identities of the clubwomen who testified.
17. Ibid., p. 4.
18. Ibid., pp. 42-43; see also p. 2.
19. *Assembly Journal*, 1905, pp. 107, 1718, 1910, 1928, 2066; *In Senate: Journals of the Proceedings of the Wisconsin Legislature* (Madison: Democrat Printing Company, 1905), pp. 1553, 1571, 1580, 1597, 1598, 1608. Hereafter cited as *Senate Journal*. La Follette had supporters among the progressively inclined clubwomen, and while governor he appointed Lucy Morris and Theodora Youmans, both former WFWC presidents, to the Wisconsin Board of Managers of the St. Louis World's Fair. La Follette's wife, Belle Case La Follette, was a clubwoman and WFWC member. I did not find, however, direct evidence of WFWC involvement in passage of the 1905 legislation.
20. Minutes, Executive Board Meeting, April 28, 1917, Wisconsin Federation of Women's Clubs Papers, Box 1, Wisconsin State Historical Society—Archives and Manuscripts Department, Madison; *Proceedings*, 1917, p. 91; *Index to the Journals of the Fifty-Third Session of the Wisconsin Legislature* (Madison:

Democrat Printing Company, 1917). pp. 380, 381, 911, 912, 913, 915 (petitions against bill 83A).

21. *Proceedings*, 1897, pp. 17-18, 37; 1898, pp. 19, 28; 1899, p. 14; 1902, pp. 39-40; 1903, p. xii; 1904, pp. 52-53.

22. *The Evening Wisconsin*, March 26, 1908, in Clippings: School Attendance, School Census and School Age, Legislative Reference Bureau, State Capitol, Madison. Hereafter cited as Clippings.

23. *Assembly Journal*, 1907, pp. 98, 486, 627-28, 1095, 1205; *Senate Journal*, 1907, pp. 587, 779, 804, 898, 957-58.

24. *Proceedings*, 1907, p. 71; Wisconsin Teachers Association, *Proceedings of the Fifty-Sixth Annual Session* (Madison: Democrat Printing Company, 1908) pp. 89, 93, 161-62; *Milwaukee Free Press*, November 14, 1908, in Clippings.

25. *Proceedings*, 1907, p. 71; 1908, p. xxv.

26. *Proceedings*, 1907, pp. 71, 72.

27. *Proceedings*, 1908, pp. 52, 73-74.

28. *Milwaukee Daily News*, March 25, 1908, and *The Evening Wisconsin*, March 26, 1908, in Clippings. Supporters of the amendment, including Ainsworth, found the opposition serious enough to consider the possibility of modifying the amendment to meet objections raised by the WFWC.

29. *Proceedings*, 1908, pp. 19, 73; 1909, pp. 32, 33, 35, 36, 44, 46, 49; *Milwaukee Sentinel*, October 9, 1908, in Clippings.

30. *Proceedings*, 1908, p. xxi; *Milwaukee Journal*, October 30, 1908, pp. 1, 15. See also *Milwaukee Sentinel*, October 24, 1908, p. 7.

31. Wisconsin Teachers Association, *Proceedings of the Fifty-Fifth Annual Session* (1907), pp. 13, 29-30.

32. Wisconsin Teachers Association, *Fifty-Sixth Annual Session* (1908), pp. 88-93; *Milwaukee Free Press*, September 10 and November 14, 1908, in Clippings.

33. Wisconsin Teachers Association, *Fifty-Sixth Annual Session*, pp. 161-62.

34. *Milwaukee Sentinel*, February 9, 1909, p. 2; *Milwaukee Daily News*, February, 2, 1909, in Clippings.

35. *Proceedings*, 1909, p. 82.

36. Wisconsin Teachers Association, *Fifty-Seventh Annual Session* (1909), p. 80. Vandewalker was the director of the Kindergarten Training Department of the Milwaukee State Normal School. She also wrote histories of the kindergarten movement, including *The Kindergarten in American Education*, published in 1908.

37. *Proceedings*, 1908, p. 73.

38. *Proceedings*, 1907, pp. 71-72.

39. *Milwaukee Sentinel*, October 25, 1908, p. 7.

40. *Proceedings*, 1908, p. 74.

41. *Milwaukee Sentinel*, October 25, 1908, part 3, p. 6.

42. *Proceedings*, 1909, pp. 83-84.

43. *Proceedings*, 1904, pp. 20-21; 1914, pp. 42, 82.

44. *Proceedings*, 1915, p. 3; Grace Abbot, "Ten Years' Work for Children," in *The United States Children's Bureau: Children and Youth: Social Problems and Social*

Policy (New York: Arno Press, 1974), p. 8; James Tobey, *The Children's Bureau: Its History, Activities and Organization* (Baltimore: Johns Hopkins Press, 1925), p. 16.

45. Abbot, "Ten Years' Work," p. 8; Tobey, *Children's Bureau*, p. 16.
46. Abbot, "Ten Years' Work," p. 8.
47. Tobey, *Children's Bureau*, pp. 12, 15.
48. Abbot, "Ten Years' Work,'" p. 8; Tobey, *Children's Bureau*, pp. 3-4, 13-15.
49. GFWC, *Official Report of the Thirteenth Biennial Convention* (1916), p. 86; United States Department of Labor, Children's Bureau, *Baby-Week Campaigns* (Washington, D.C.: Government Printing Office, 1917), pp. 9, 28; *Proceedings*, 1915, pp. 3, 8.
50. *Proceedings*, 1915, pp. 30-31.
51. *Proceedings*, 1909, p. 28; 1911, pp. xxiv, xxxiii; 1912, p. xxix; 1913, p. 49; 1914, pp. 32-33; 1915, p. 41.
52. Brief accounts of Baby Week celebrations can be found in the district reports at the 1916 convention. For a more detailed account of a Baby Week celebration in a small town (about 2,000 inhabitants), see Minutes, 1913-1921, River Falls Tuesday Club Records, Box 1, volume 3, December 6, 1915-April 25, 1916, Wisconsin State Historical Society—River Falls Area Research Center; *River Falls Journal*, February 10, 1916, p. 1; February 17, 1916, pp. 4, 10; February 24, 1916, p. 1; March 2, 1916, pp. 1, 4; March 9, 1916 p. 1; March 16, 1916, p. 4. For accounts of Baby Week in Wisconsin's largest city, Milwaukee, see *Proceedings*, 1916, pp. 102-3; *Milwaukee Sentinel*, May 15, 1916, pp. 1-2; May 16, 1916, pp. 1, 21; May 18, 1916, p. 3; May 21, 1916, p. 2.
53. Baby contests awarded prizes to the "healthiest babies," based on measures such as weight. The award-winning babies in Milwaukee's contest may have disappointed the organizers of Baby Week, who were trying to convince the public of the value of expert advice. According to the *Milwaukee Sentinel* account, the mothers of the winners said that the babies were "not reared on new-fangled ideas" but "just grew that way." One of these mothers declared, "I raised this baby to suit myself. . . . I didn't listen to any faddish rules or read any books on how to raise a baby. I raised him myself and I guess I haven't made a failure of it." *Milwaukee Sentinel*, May 18, 1916, p. 3.
54. *Proceedings*, 1916, pp. 79, 90-91; Department of Labor, *Baby-Week Campaigns*, p. 27.
55. *Proceedings*, 1915, p. 80, 103-5; Department of Labor, *Baby-Week Campaigns*, p. 9; Minutes, Conference of Officers, February 1, 1916, WFWC Papers, Box 1.
56. *Proceedings*, 1916, p. 51; Department of Labor, *Baby-Week Campaigns*, p. 27; Minutes, Conference of Officers, February 1, 1916, WFWC Papers, Box 1.
57. Department of Labor, *Baby-Week Campaigns*, p. 30. These "interested women" may well have been members of unfederated clubs.
58. *Proceedings*, 1915, p. 105; 1916, p. 51; *Milwaukee Sentinel*, May 15, 1916, p. 1; Department of Labor, *Baby-Week Campaigns*, p. 30.

59. *Proceedings*, 1916, p. 51, 102-3. The material on the River Falls and Milwaukee Baby Weeks (see above) offers good examples of cooperation and joint efforts. In River Falls, three women's clubs organized the Baby Week event. They had local physicians give lectures and lend them equipment for the baby contest; arranged programs at the high school and normal schools, holding the baby contest in the kindergarten room; convinced newspapers to donate advertising space; and prevailed on local ministers to give sermons on Baby Week. The committee coordinating Milwaukee's Baby Week was chaired by a local physician and had Milwaukee's commissioner of health on it, as well as clubwomen. A variety of organizations set up booths and exhibits in the large auditorium that housed the Baby Week activities.

60. *Proceedings*, 1916, pp. 51, 102-3.

61. Department of Labor, *Baby-Week Celebrations*, p. 30.

62. Information on just how well attended Baby Week events were is difficult to find. In Milwaukee, estimates ranged from 40,000 to 50,000 people.

63. *Proceedings*, 1917, pp. 48, 50, 73, 80-83.

64. Tobey, *Children's Bureau*, pp. 8, 17; Abbot, "Ten Years' Work," p. 9.

65. *Proceedings*, 1916, pp. 8-9, 79, 102-5.

66. Ibid., p. 103. As a result of Baby Week, the River Falls Tuesday Club organized a Community Welfare Committee, which obtained a visiting nurse for River Falls, and organized a local affiliate of the Wisconsin Anti-Tuberculosis Association. District reports in 1916 and 1917 are sprinkled with club accounts of similar activity.

67. Discussions of the Sheppard-Towner Act can be found in Rothman, *Woman's Proper Place*, pp. 136-53; Chafe, *The American Woman*, pp. 27-28.

68. Abbot, "Ten Years' Work," p. 9.

CHAPTER FOUR

1. Many were found in the *Wisconsin Necrology*, a bound file of obituaries of prominent Wisconsin residents, at the Wisconsin State Historical Society, Madison.

2. U.S. Bureau of the Census, *Sixteenth Census of the United States: 1940. Population. Characteristics by Age*, volume 4, part 4, p. 881. The 1940 census was the first census that asked for years of school completed. Of women fifty-five years or older at the time of this census—those born no later than 1883—4.6 percent reported completing at least one year of college. Of course, many women in this age group were dead by the 1940 census and so did not appear in the figures. It is unlikely that college-educated women died at a greater rate than non-college-educated women, and because of class differences between those who attend college and those who do not, one would suspect that, if anything, college-educated women lived longer than women without advanced schooling. So 4.6 percent possibly overestimates the proportion of Wisconsin women born

by 1885 who attended college, and almost certainly does not underestimate this proportion.

3. See Robert V. Wells, "Women's Lives Transformed: Demographic and Family Patterns in America, 1600-1970," in Carol Berkin and Mary Beth Norton, eds., *Women of America: A History* (Boston: Houghton Mifflin, 1979), p. 20; U.S. Bureau of the Census, *Historical Statistics of the United States: Colonial Times to 1970* (Washington, D.C.: Government Printing Office, 1975), part 1, p. 19.

4. This is definitely true for Caroline Tichenor, and probably true for Jennie Bardon. See *Waupun Leader*, October 20, 1909, p. 1; and *Ashland Press*, November 22, 1939, in *Wisconsin Necrology*, vol. 42, pp. 18-19. One of the difficulties of the obituaries is that they infrequently give the date a woman joined a particular organization, so it is difficult to assess specifically which types of activities were the most likely point of entry into the public realm for WFWC leaders. Anne Firor Scott has argued that church work played this role in the lives of southern women after the Civil War. *The Southern Lady: From Pedestal to Politics, 1830-1930* (Chicago: University of Chicago Press, 1970), pp. 135-44.

5. On Strathearn, see "Forty-Two Years . . . And More," *The Wisconsin Clubwoman*, vol. 22, November/December, 1939, pp. 30-31. On Hooper, see "Biography," Jessie Jack Hooper Papers, Box 21, p. 7, Wisconsin State Historical Society—Archives and Manuscripts Department, Madison.

6. Mary Hobbins, Ione Wright, Jennie Estabrook, Carrie Edwards, and Martha Buell.

7. Edna Chynoweth, Lucy Morris, Ellen Sabin, Theodora Youmans, Lutie Stearns, Mary Bradford, Emma Crosby, Sophie Gudden, Rose Swart, Sophie Strathearn, Vie Campbell, Lettie Harvey, Emma Conley, Eva Pease, Charlotte Witter, Abby Marlatt, Mary Rote, and Jessie Jack Hooper.

8. The plaque named Edna Chynoweth, Jessie Jack Hooper, Lucy Morris, Ellen Sabin, and Theodora Youmans. It also included a clubwoman named Rachel Jastrow, of Madison, who was active in the WFWC but did not quite fit the criteria established to define a leader.

9. WCTU members included Vie Campbell, Lutie Stearns, Edna Chynoweth, and Adalaide Magee. Sophie Gudden, Sophie Strathearn and Vie Campbell belonged to the Consumers' League. Supporters of the peace movement included Lucy Morris, Lutie Stearns, Jessie Jack Hooper, and Edna Chynoweth.

10. See *Eau Claire Leader*, July 25, 1951, p. 6, and *Wisconsin State Journal*, December 20, 1926, in *Wisconsin Necrology*, vol. 24, pp. 114-15.

11. Hobbins was an ardent antisuffragist, which the editors failed to mention. Interestingly, she did at least her hospital work with Rachel Jastrow, an equally ardent prosuffragist. For Hobbins's obituary, see *Capital Times*, July 15, 1935, and *Wisconsin State Journal*, July 19, 1935, in *Wisconsin Necrology*, vol. 35, pp. 230, 234.

12. Andrea Bletzinger and Anne Short, eds., *Wisconsin Woman: A Gifted Heritage* (project of the American Association of University Women—Wisconsin State Division, n.p., 1982), p. 42.

13. Lutie Stearns, "Mrs. Morris and the Library Movement," *The Wisconsin Clubwoman*, vol. 12, April 1929, p. 55.

14. See *Proceedings*, 1909, p. 4.

15. The best sources on Morris are *Milwaukee Sentinel*, May 28, 1935, in *Wisconsin Necrology*, vol. 35, pp. 186-87; Bletzinger and Short, *Wisconsin Woman*, pp. 40-42. On Morris's war work, see McCaul, "Wisconsin Women's War Work," pp. 7, 38.

16. On Neville, see her extensive obituary in *Green Bay Gazette*, July 8, 1935, in *Wisconsin Necrology*, vol. 35, pp. 224-25. See also "Memorial to Mrs. Arthur Courteney Neville," *The Wisconsin Clubwoman*, vol. 18, September 1935, p. 123; Ruth Kohler, *The Story of Wisconsin Women* (Committee on Wisconsin Women for the 1948 Wisconsin Centennial, n.p., 1948), p. 91.

17. *Whitewater Press*, April 18, 1940, in *Wisconsin Necrology*, vol. 42, p. 247; *Whitewater Register*, December 1, 1952, p. 1.

18. For Crosby's obituary, see *Racine Journal-Times*, January 19, 1951, pp. 1-2. Crosby's leadership in the DAR included a national vice-presidency in 1917. She also founded and led a local chapter.

19. On Crosby's suffrage service, see Dr. G. B. Willis to Crystal Eastman Benedict, letter, September 28, 1912, Ada James Papers, Box 15, folder—September 28-30, 1912, Wisconsin State Historical Society—Archives and Manuscripts Department, Madison.

20. Della Emerson's obituary may be found in *Beloit News*, February 7, 1938, in *Wisconsin Necrology*, vol. 39, pp. 190-91. On her husband, see *Beloit News*, February 6, 1939, in *Wisconsin Necrology*, vol. 41, p. 9.

21. See *Proceedings*, 1910, p. 9. On her antisuffragism see Sophie Gudden to Ada James, letter, October 3, 1912, Ada James Papers, Box 15, folder—October 1-13, 1912.

22. On Carrie Edwards, see *Oshkosh Daily Northwestern*, February 27, 1939, p. 4; *Bunn's Oshkosh Directory* (Oshkosh: John V. Bunn), 1989, p. 8, and 1908, p. 22. On her husband, see *Oshkosh Northwestern*, June 2, 1943, in *Wisconsin Necrology*, vol. 49, p. 52.

23. Summaries of Sabin's career may be found in Fred Holmes, ed., *Wisconsin: Stability * Progress * Beauty* (Chicago: Lewis Publishing Company, 1946), vol. 5, pp. 47-48; Women's Auxiliary of the Wisconsin State Historical Society, *Famous Wisconsin Women* (n.p., 1976), vol. 6, pp. 55-58; Edward T. James, et al., *Notable American Women* (Cambridge, MA: Harvard University Press, 1971), vol. 3, pp. 217-18.

24. Women's Auxiliary, *Famous Wisconsin Women*, vol. 6, p. 58; James, *Notable American Women*, vol. 3, p. 217.

25. Summaries of Bradford's career can be found in *Kenosha News*, February 4, 1943, in *Wisconsin Necrology*, vol. 48, pp. 188-89; John Gregory, ed., *Southeastern Wisconsin: A History of Old Milwaukee County* (Chicago: S. J. Clarke, 1932), vol. 4, pp. 154-65.

26. On criticism of Bradford, see Gregory, *Southeastern Wisconsin*, vol. 4, pp. 161-62.

27. See especially, *Proceedings*, 1905, pp. 63-64; 1906, pp. 55-58.

28. *Wisconsin State Journal*, June 24, 1943, in *Wisconsin Necrology*, vol. 49, pp. 103-4; James, *Notable American Women*, vol. 2, p. 496.

29. Durward Howes, ed., *American Women, 1935-1940* (Detroit: Gale Research, 1981), vol. 2, p. 565; James, *Notable American Women*, vol. 2, p. 496; *Proceedings*, 1916, p. 88.

30. Stearns's library career is well documented. See Wisconsin Historical Society, *Dictionary of Wisconsin Biography*, (Milwaukee: Northern American Press, 1960) p. 337; Victoria Brown, *The Uncommon Lives of Common Women: The Missing Half of Wisconsin History* (Wisconsin Feminists Project Fund, Inc., n.p., 1975), pp. 44-45; James, *Notable American Women*, vol. 3, p. 353; Lutie Stearns, "My Seventy-Five Years: Part I, 1866-1914," *Wisconsin Magazine of History* 42 (Spring 1959): 214-18.

31. Stearns, "Mrs. Morris and the Library Movement," p. 55; Kohler, *Wisconsin Women*, p. 88.

32. Brown, *Uncommon Lives*, p. 44, refers to Stearns's "staff of one." On Stearns's club work generally, see Howes, *American Women*, vol. 2, p. 860; "Federation Founders," pp. 13, 33. The best information on Stearns's use of club contacts to promote libraries is found in club reports at conventions, which mention her talks at club meetings and district conventions, and the help she gave to clubs that were organizing community libraries. See, for example, *Proceedings*, 1898, p. 48; 1908, p. 20; 1913, p. 89.

33. *Milwaukee Sentinel*, January 4, 1921, and *Oconomowoc Enterprise*, January 7, 1921, in *Wisconsin Necrology*, pp. 228-29, 231; *Proceedings*, 1905, p. 46. See also Julia Lapham's papers in Increase Lapham Papers, Boxes 21 and 22, Wisconsin State Historical Society—Archives and Manuscripts Department, Madison. Julia Lapham's papers, consisting mostly of letters, contain information on the types of activities that constituted her contributions to historical study and preservation.

34. H. M. Quaife, *Wisconsin: Its History and Its People, 1863-1924* (Chicago: S. J. Clarke, 1924), vol. 1, pp. 386-89.

35. Graves, "Wisconsin Woman Suffrage Movement," p. 371; *Proceedings*, 1905, p. 69; Vie Campbell to Theodora Youmans, undated letter, Wisconsin Woman Suffrage Association Papers, Box 11, file—1916, Wisconsin State Historical Society—Archives and Manuscripts Department, Madison; Woman's Christian Temperance Union of Wisconsin, *Annual Reports* (1892-1907). See lists of officers contained in each report. On Campbell's prosuffrage sentiments, see WCTU Report for 1895, pp. 58-66; see 1895, pp. 52-54 on workers.

36. Brown, *Uncommon Lives*, p. 20; Kohler, *Wisconsin Women*, p. 35; Graves, "Wisconsin Woman Suffrage Movement," pp. 99, 230, 377; Alice Bleyer to Alice Curtis, letter, February 5, 1915, Wisconsin Woman Suffrage Association Papers, Box 6, file—February 1915.

37. Graves, "Wisconsin Woman Suffrage Movement," p. 361; *Proceedings*, 1904, p. 6.

38. "Federation Founders," p. 13.
39. See especially, Howes, *American Women*, vol. 2, p. 860; Brown, *Uncommon Lives*, p. 45; "Federation Founders," pp. 13, 33; James, *Notable American Women*, vol. 3, p. 354; Lutie Stearns, "My Seventy-Five Years, Part II, 1914-1942," *Wisconsin Magazine of History* 42 (Summer 1959): 282-87; Lutie Stearns, "My Seventy-Five Years, Part III, Increasingly Personal," *Wisconsin Magazine of History* 43 (Winter 1959-1960): 97-101. *Proceedings*, 1913, pp. 66, 75, 77.
40. Much of the information on Sophie Gudden comes from letters she wrote during the course of the suffrage campaign. See Ada James Papers, Boxes 6, 7, and 15; and Wisconsin Woman Suffrage Association Papers, Boxes 6, 10, and 11. See also, Kohler, *Wisconsin Women*, p. 120; Graves, "Wisconsin Woman Suffrage Movement," pp. 112, 143, 174, 176, 180; Maud Nathan, *Story of an Epoch Making Movement* (Garden City, NY: Doubleday, 1926), p. 222. WFWC convention reports also provide excellent examples of Gudden's use of Federation work to advance Consumers' League and suffrage interests. See *Proceedings*, 1903, pp. xv, 23-24, 37-38; 1904, p. xiv; 1905, p. xix; 1908, p. 49; 1909, pp. 35-36, 65-66; 1910, p. 71; 1911, pp. xxxiii, 23, 71; 1912, p. 76; 1913, p. 122. Also along these lines see: Sophie Gudden to Ada James, letter, July 23, 1911, Ada James Papers, Box 6, folder—July-August 15, 1911; Sophie Gudden to Anna Shaw, letter, November 16, 1911, Ada James Papers, Box 6, folder—October 1-November, 1911.
41. Sophie Gudden to Ada James, letter, January 29, 1912, Ada James Papers, Box 7, folder—January 1912.
42. On Connor, see *Wisconsin State Journal*, December 20, 1926, in *Wisconsin Necrology*, vol. 24, pp. 114-15; Kohler, *Wisconsin Women*, p. 98; *Wisconsin Alumni Directory, 1849-1919* (1921), University of Wisconsin Archives, Madison.
43. For Chandler's obituary, see *Racine Journal Times*, September 9, 1933, in *Wisconsin Necrology*, vol. 33, pp. 34-35. See also *The Wisconsin Clubwoman*, vol. 16, September 1933, p. 132, and vol. 16, November 1933, pp. 167-68.
44. On Strathearn's leadership in her local club, see Minutes, 1894-1906 and yearbooks, 1901-1977, Kaukauna Woman's Club Records, Boxes 1 and 3, Wisconsin State Historical Society—Green Bay Area Research Center.
45. On Strathearn's work in the Wisconsin Consumers' League and Woman's Relief's Corps, see "Forty Two Years . . . And More," pp. 30-31. In 1911, Strathearn wrote Wisconsin State Senator David James and asked him for help in securing the appointment. She noted that she had "some fine endorsements filed" but "the political situation is perplexing." Strathearn addressed James as "Comrade James," probably because of his membership in the Grand Army of the Republic, with which the WRC was associated. I do not know whether James helped her or not, but the appointment went to another woman. See Sophie Strathearn to "Comrade James," letter, February 13, 1911, Ada James Papers, Box 5, folder—January-March 1911.
46. Information on Strathearn's activities past 1920 can be found in Howes, *American Women*, vol. 2, p. 875; *Manitowoc Herald-Times*, August 24, 1948, p. 2.

47. When president of the WFWC at the turn of the century, Youmans carefully but firmly pressured clubwomen to use their school suffrage. She also was instrumental in obtaining the WFWC's endorsement of suffrage. On Youmans's suffrage work, see *Waukesha Daily Freeman*, August 17, 1932, in *Wisconsin Necrology*, vol. 31, pp. 134-36; and Women's Auxiliary, *Famous Wisconsin Women*, vol. 1, pp. 15-16. Information on Youmans also can be found in Graves, "Wisconsin Woman Suffrage Movement," pp. 142, 146, 246, and throughout the Ada James Papers and the Wisconsin Woman Suffrage Association Papers.

48. See *Waukesha Daily Freeman*, August 17, 1932, in *Wisconsin Necrology*, vol. 31, pp. 134-36; Graves, "Wisconsin Woman Suffrage Movement," p. 360.

49. *Waukesha Daily Freeman*, August 17, 1932, in *Wisconsin Necrology*, vol. 31, pp. 134-36.

50. On Hooper's activities in Oshkosh, see *Oshkosh Daily Northwestern*, May 8, 1935, and *Milwaukee Sentinel*, May 19, 1935, in *Wisconsin Necrology*, vol. 35, pp. 164-65; James, *Notable American Women*, vol. 2, pp. 215-16; Biography, Jessie Jack Hooper Papers, Box 21, pp. 6-11.

51. On Hooper's suffrage work, see *Oshkosh Daily Northwestern*, May 8, 1935, in *Wisconsin Necrology*, vol. 35, pp. 163-64; James, *Notable American Women*, vol. 2, p. 216; Bletzinger and Short, *Wisconsin Woman*, p. 64; Charlotte Witter to Theodora Youmans, letter, September 16, 1916, Wisconsin Woman Suffrage Association Papers, Box 11, folder—September 1916.

52. McCaul, *Wisconsin Women's War Work*, pp. 3, 36; James, *Notable American Women*, vol. 2, p. 216.

53. See Women's Auxiliary, *Famous Wisconsin Women*, vol. 4, p. 31.

54. On Hooper's peace and political activities, see *Oshkosh Daily Northwestern*, May 8, 1935, in *Wisconsin Necrology*, vol. 35, pp. 163-64; James, *Notable American Women*, p. 216; Bletzinger and Short, *Wisconsin Woman*, pp. 64-65.

55. Sophie Gudden to Ada James, letter, September 20, 1912, Ada James Papers, Box 15, folder—Sept. 17-20, 1912.

56. Theodora Youmans to Ada James, letter, December 1911, Ada James Papers, Box 7.

57. *Oshkosh Northwestern*, November 25, 1910, in *Wisconsin Necrology*, vol. 12, p. 20.

58. *Monroe Times*, February 22, 1926, in *Wisconsin Necrology*, vol. 23, pp. 218-19.

SUMMARY

1. *Proceedings*, 1912, p. 96.

Bibliography

PRIMARY SOURCES

Manuscript Collections

Wisconsin State Historical Society, Archives and Manuscripts Department, Madison. Ada James Papers, Increase Lapham Papers, "Information about Mary Davison Bradford," Jessie Jack Hooper Papers, Wisconsin Federation of Women's Clubs Papers, Wisconsin Woman Suffrage Association Papers.
Wisconsin State Historical Society, Green Bay Area Research Center, Green Bay. Kaukauna Woman's Club Records.
Wisconsin State Historical Society, River Falls Area Research Center, River Falls. River Falls Improvement League Records, River Falls Tuesday Club Papers.

Census

United States Bureau of the Census. *Historical Statistics of the United States: Colonial Times to 1970*. Part 1. Washington, D.C.: Government Printing Office, 1975.
United States Bureau of the Census. *Manuscript Schedules of the Population*. 1900.
United States Bureau of the Census. *Religious Bodies, Part 1, 1906*. Washington, D.C.: Government Printing Office, 1910.
United States Bureau of the Census. *Sixteenth Census of the United States: 1940. Population. Differential Fertility, 1940 and 1910: Fertility for States and Large Cities*. Washington, D.C.: Government Printing Office, 1943.
United States Bureau of the Census. *Sixteenth Census of the United States: 1940. Population. Characteristics by Age*. Volume 4, part 4. Washington, D.C.: Government Printing Office, 1943.

United States Bureau of the Census. *Thirteenth Census of the United States: 1910 Abstract with Supplement for Wisconsin.* Washington, D.C.: Government Printing Office, 1913.

Wisconsin, Department of State. *Manuscript Schedules of the Population.* 1905.

Magazines and Newspapers

Annals of the American Academy of Political and Social Science 28 (September 1906).

Antigo Journal, October 31, 1928.

Appleton Post-Crescent, February 21, 1915.

Ashland Press, February 2, 1923; November 22, 1939.

Beliot News, February 7, 1938; February 6, 1939.

Capital Times, July 15, August 4, 1935; January 13, 1937; February 7, 1938; October 9, 1942.

Eau Claire Leader, December 15, 1925; July 24, July 25, 1951.

Evening Wisconsin, March 26, 1908.

Fond du Lac Commonwealth, June 22, 1922.

Fond du Lac Commonwealth Reporter, February 28, 1933; March 8, 1943.

Fond du Lac Reporter, October 1, 1929.

Green Bay Gazette, June 27, 1921; May 20, 1929; July 8, 1935.

Janesville Gazette, May 9, 1929.

Kenosha News, February 4, 1943.

Madison Democrat, October 16, 1906; November 14, 1916; December 4, 1918; August 31, 1920.

Manitowoc Herald-Times, August 24, 1948.

Milwaukee Daily News, March 25, 1908; February 2, 1909.

Milwaukee Free Press, September 20, November 14, 1908.

Milwaukee Journal, October 30, 1908; June 6, 1932.

Milwaukee Sentinel, June 19, October 9, October 24, October 25, 1908; February 9, 1909; May, 1916; January 4, 1921; January 23, 1928; May 6, 1935; May 19, May 28, 1935.

Monroe Evening Times, July 27, 1921.

Monroe Times, February 22, 1926.

Neenah-Menasha Daily News Times, February 26, 1931.

Oconomowoc Enterprise, January 7, 1921.

Oshkosh Northwestern. November 25, 1910; June 2, 1922; April 23, 1927; February 11, 1930; May 8, 1935; February 27, 1939; December 21, 1939; April 16, 1943; June 2, 1943.
Portage Democrat, December 13, 1928.
Racine Journal-Times, January 21, 1924; September 9, 1933; January 19, 1951.
Reedsburg Times-Press, March 9, 1944.
Rhinelander Daily News, April 25, 1923.
River Falls Journal, February and March 1916.
River Falls Morning Sentinel, June 11, 1942.
Stoughton Hub, September 11, 1926.
Tomah Journal, January 1, 1942.
Waukesha Daily Freeman, January 21, 1931; August 17, 1932.
Waupun Leader, October 20, 1909.
Wausau Daily Record Herald, December 7, 1925; March 11, 1937.
Wausau Pilot, December 10, 1925.
Whitewater Press, April 18, 1940.
Whitewater Register, December 1, 1952.
Wisconsin Alumni Magazine, vol. 1.
Wisconsin Citizen, vols. 27, 28.
Wisconsin Clubwoman, vols. 1-34.
Wisconsin Rapids Tribune, September 26, 1942.
Wisconsin State Journal, December 20, 1926; July 19, 1935; October 6, 1940; April 2, 1942; June 24, 1943.

Printed Proceedings and Reports of Meetings

General Federation of Women's Clubs. *Proceedings of the Biennial Conventions.* Various places and publishers, 1896-1916.
In Assembly: Journal of the Proceedings of the Wisconsin Legislature. Madison: Democrat Printing Company, 1905, 1907.
In Senate: Journals of the Proceedings of the Wisconsin Legislature. Madison: Democrat Printing Company, 1907.
Index to the Journals of the Fifty-Third Session of the Wisconsin Legislature. Madison: Democrat Printing Company, 1917.
Wisconsin State Federation of Women's Clubs. *Proceedings of the Annual Conventions.* Various publishers and places, 1897-1917.

Wisconsin Teachers Association. *Proceedings of the Annual Sessions*. Madison: Democrat Printing Company, 1907-1909.

Woman's Christian Temperance Union. *Annual Reports*. Various places and publishers, 1892-1907.

Miscellaneous

Blue Book of the State of Wisconsin. Milwaukee: Henry Gugler, 1897.

Croly, Jane Cunningham. *The History of the Woman's Club Movement in America*. New York: Henry G. Allen, 1898.

Madison, Wisconsin City Directory. N.p., 1917.

Philippi's Souvenir Directory of the City of La Crosse. La Crosse: L. P. Philippi Company, 1900, 1905, 1909.

Portrait and Biographical Album of Rock County Wisconsin. Chicago: Acme Publishing, 1889.

R. L. Polk and Company's Ashland Directory. St. Paul, MN: R. L. Polk & Company, 1897, 1905, 1909.

Lutie Stearns, "My Seventy-Five Years, Part I, 1866-1914," *Wisconsin Magazine of History* 42 (Spring 1959): 211-18.

Lutie Stearns, "My Seventy-Five Years, Part II, 1914-1942," *Wisconsin Magazine of History* 42 (Summer 1959): 282-87.

Lutie Stearns, "My Seventy-Five Years, Part III, Increasingly Personal," *Wisconsin Magazine of History* 43 (Winter 1959-1960): 97-105.

United States Department of Labor, Children's Bureau. *Baby Week Campaigns*. Rev. ed. Washington, D.C.: Government Printing Office, 1919.

Wisconsin Alumni Directory, 1849-1919 (1921). University of Wisconsin Archives, Madison.

Wood, Mary I. *The History of the General Federation of Women's Clubs for the First Twenty-Two Years of Its Organization*. New York: General Federation of Women's Clubs, 1912.

Wright's Directory of Fond du Lac County. Milwaukee: A. G. Wright, 1901.

Wright's Directory of Rhinelander and Oneida County. Milwaukee: Wright Directory Company, 1921.

SECONDARY SOURCES

Abbott, Grace, "Ten Years' Work for Children." *The U.S. Children's Bureau, 1912-1972. Children and Youth: Social Problems and Social Policy*. New York: Arno Press, 1974.

Ault, Nelson A. "The Earnest Ladies: The Walla Walla Woman's Club and the Equal Suffrage League of 1886-1889," *Pacific Northwest Quarterly* 42 (April 1951): 123-37.

Beard, Mary Ritter. *Woman's Work in Municipalities*. New York: D. Appleton, 1915.

Blair, Karen J. *The Clubwoman as Feminist: True Womanhood Redefined, 1868-1914*. New York: Holmes & Meier, 1980.

Bletzinger, Andrea and Anne Short, eds., *Wisconsin Woman: A Gifted Heritage*. A project of the American Association of University Women—Wisconsin State Division. N.p., 1982.

Bordin, Ruth. *Woman and Temperance: The Quest for Power and Liberty, 1873-1900*. Philadelphia: Temple University Press, 1981.

Breckinridge, Sophonisba P. *Women in the Twentieth Century: A Study of Their Political, Social and Economic Activities*. New York: McGraw-Hill, 1933.

Brown, Victoria. *The Uncommon Lives of Common Women: The Missing Half of Wisconsin History*. Wisconsin Feminists Project Fund, Inc., N.p., 1975.

Chafe, William. *The American Woman: Her Changing Social, Economic and Political Roles, 1920-1970*. New York: Oxford University Press, 1972.

Conway, Jill. "Women Reformers and American Culture, 1870-1930." *Our American Sisters: Women in American Life and Thought*, ed. Jean E. Friedman and William G. Shade. Boston: Allyn and Bacon, 1973, pp. 301-12.

Epstein, Barbara Leslie. *The Politics of Domesticity: Women, Evangelism and Temperance in Nineteenth Century America*. Middletown, CT: Wesleyan University Press, 1981.

Freedman, Estelle. "Separatism as Strategy: Female Institution Building and American Feminism, 1870-1930." *Feminist Studies* 5 (Fall 1979): pp. 512-28.

Graves, Lawrence. "The Wisconsin Woman Suffrage Movement, 1846-1920." Ph.D. dissertation, University of Wisconsin, 1954.

Gregory, John, ed. *Southeastern Wisconsin: A History of Old Milwaukee County*. Chicago: S. J. Clarke, 1932.

Gregory, John, ed. *Southeastern Wisconsin: A History of Old Crawford County*. Chicago: S. J. Clarke, 1932.

Holmes, Fred, ed. *Wisconsin: Stability * Progress * Beauty*. Chicago: Lewis Publishing Company, 1946.

Howes, Durward, ed. *American Women, 1935-1940: A Composite Biographical Dictionary*. Detroit: Gale Research, 1981.

James, Edward T., et al., eds. *Notable American Women*. Cambridge, MA: Harvard University Press, 1971.

Kohler, Ruth. *The Story of Wisconsin Women*. Committee on Wisconsin Women for the 1948 Wisconsin Centennial, n.p., 1948.

Lawson, Publius, ed. *History of Winnebago County*. Chicago: C. F. Cooper Company, 1908.

Lerner, Gerda. "Community Work of Black Club Women." *The Majority Finds Its Past*. Gerda Lerner, ed. New York: Oxford University Press, 1979, pp. 83-93.

McCaul, Alice Louise. "Wisconsin Women's War Work." Bachelor's thesis, University of Wisconsin, 1930.

Nathan, Maud. *Story of an Epoch Making Movement*. Garden City, NY: Doubleday, 1926.

O'Neill, William. *Everyone Was Brave: The Rise and Fall of Feminism in America*. Chicago: Quadrangle Books, 1969.

Quaife, H. M. *Wisconsin: Its History and Its People, 1863-1924*. Chicago: S.J. Clarke, 1924.

Rothman, Sheila. *Woman's Proper Place: A History of Changing Ideals and Practices, 1870 to the Present*. New York: Basic Books, 1978.

Scott, Anne Firor. *The Southern Lady: From Pedestal to Politics, 1830-1930*. Chicago: University of Chicago Press, 1970.

Seybold, Charlotte Reid. "The Waukesha County Historical Society," *Wisconsin Magazine of History* 32 (Winter 1948-1949): pp. 49-57.

Tobey, James. *The Children's Bureau: Its History, Activities and Organization*. Baltimore: Johns Hopkins Press, 1925.

Usher, Ellis Baker. *Wisconsin: Its Story and Biography, 1848-1913*. Chicago: Lewis Publishing Company, 1914.

Wells, Mildred White. *Unity in Diversity: The History of the General Federation of Women's Clubs*. Washington, D.C.: General Federation of Women's Clubs, 1953.

Wells, Robert V. "Women's Lives Transformed: Demographic and Family Patterns in America, 1600-1970." *Women of America: A History*, ed. Carol

Berkin and Mary Beth Norton. Boston: Houghton Mifflin, 1979, pp. 17-33.

Who Was Who in America. Chicago: A. N. Marquis, 1950.

Wisconsin Historical Society. *Dictionary of Wisconsin Biography*. Milwaukee: North American Press, 1960.

Women's Auxiliary of the Wisconsin State Historical Society. *Famous Wisconsin Women*. n. p., 1976.

Index

Scholarship in Women's History: Rediscovered and New

GERDA LERNER, Editor